King Alfr... ...fessor of English at Oxford University. He is a distinguished critic, reviewer and broadcaster, and the author of several books, including *The Intellectuals and the Masses*. He is also the editor of *The Faber Book of Reportage*, *The Faber Book of Science* and, most recently, *The Faber Book of Utopias*.

Pure Pleasure

*A Guide to the Twentieth Century's
Most Enjoyable Books*

JOHN CAREY

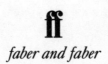

faber and faber

First published in Great Britain in 2000
by Faber and Faber Limited
3 Queen Square London WC1N 3AU

Typeset by Faber and Faber Ltd
Printed in England by Mackays of Chatham plc Kent

© John Carey, 2000

John Carey is hereby identified as author of this
work in accordance with Section 77 of the Copyright,
Designs and Patents Act 1988

A CIP record for this book
is available from the British Library

ISBN 0–571–20448–1

2 4 6 8 10 9 7 5 3

Contents

Why Read? A Polemical Introduction ix

A. Conan Doyle, *The Hound of the Baskervilles*, 1902 1

André Gide, *The Immoralist*, 1902 4

Rudyard Kipling, *Traffics and Discoveries*, 1904 8

Joseph Conrad, *The Secret Agent*, 1907 11

E. M. Forster, *A Room with a View*, 1908 14

G. K. Chesterton, *The Man Who Was Thursday*, 1908 17

Arnold Bennett, *The Old Wives' Tale*, 1908 20

H. G. Wells, *The History of Mr Polly*, 1910 23

Maxim Gorky, *My Childhood*, 1913 26

Thomas Hardy, *Satires of Circumstance*, 1914 30

James Joyce, *A Portrait of the Artist as a Young Man*,
 1916 34

D. H. Lawrence, *Twilight in Italy*, 1916 37

T. S. Eliot, *Prufrock and Other Observations*, 1917 40

Edward Thomas (d. 1917), *Collected Poems*, 1936 44

Katherine Mansfield, *The Garden Party*, 1922 48

Jaroslav Hašek (d. 1923), *The Good Soldier Svejk*, 1930   51

Aldous Huxley, *Those Barren Leaves*, 1925   55

F. Scott Fitzgerald, *The Great Gatsby*, 1925   58

Mikhail Bulgakov, *A Country Doctor's Notebook*,
    1925–7   61

Sylvia Townsend Warner, *Mr Fortune's Maggot*, 1927   64

Evelyn Waugh, *Decline and Fall*, 1928   67

Robert Graves, *Goodbye to All That*, 1929   71

William Empson, *Seven Types of Ambiguity*, 1930   74

W. B. Yeats, *Collected Poems*, 1933   77

Christopher Isherwood, *Mr Norris Changes Trains*,
    1935   81

Elizabeth Bowen, *The House in Paris*, 1935   85

John Steinbeck, *Of Mice and Men*, 1937   88

Graham Greene, *Brighton Rock*, 1938   91

A. E. Housman, *Collected Poems*, 1939   94

George Orwell, *Coming Up for Air*, 1939   98

Keith Douglas, *Alamein to Zem Zem*, 1946   101

Thomas Mann, *Confessions of Felix Krull,
    Confidence Man*, 1954   105

Kingsley Amis, *Lucky Jim*, 1954   108

William Golding, *The Inheritors*, 1955   112

V. S. Naipaul, *The Mystic Masseur*, 1957   115

vi

S. J. Perelman, *The Road to Miltown, or Under the
   Spreading Atrophy*, 1957   118

W. H. Auden, *Collected Shorter Poems 1927–57*,
   1966   122

Günter Grass, *The Tin Drum*, 1959   126

Muriel Spark, *The Prime of Miss Jean Brodie*, 1961   129

Jean-Paul Sartre, *Words*, 1964   132

Seamus Heaney, *Death of a Naturalist*, 1966   135

Stevie Smith, *The Frog Prince and Other Poems*, 1966   138

Ted Hughes, *Crow: From the Life and Songs of
   Crow*, 1970   142

Ian McEwan, *The Cement Garden*, 1978   146

Clive James, *Unreliable Memoirs*, 1980   149

John Updike, *A Rabbit Omnibus* (1960–82), 1991   152

Philip Larkin, *Collected Poems*, 1988   155

Vikram Seth, *A Suitable Boy*, 1993   159

Kazuo Ishiguro, *The Unconsoled*, 1995   163

Graham Swift, *Last Orders*, 1996   166

Afterwards: *A Books-Choice Postbag*   169

Acknowledgements   175

Why Read?
A Polemical Introduction

Will there still be books by the end of the next millennium? It sounds an alarmist question, but it is serious. If you go back a thousand years, it was not exactly a big scene bookwise. Most people were illiterate. Printing had not been invented. At the end of another thousand years, things may be just as remote from anything we can imagine now. In H. G. Wells's novel *When the Sleeper Wakes*, a character called Graham comes out of a cataleptic trance in the year 2200 and finds that books are already obsolete. They have been replaced by videos, played on television screens (called 'kinetoscopes'), and labelled in crude phonetic English, which is all anyone can manage to write.

When I was starting out on this project, the news came through that literature was to have no place in the Millennium Dome. Presumably that amounts to an official, Blairite judgement that reading is on the way out, if not dead already, so far as the majority are concerned. That could be right. But it could also be seriously wrong. The Dome is an anachronism because, if it succeeds, it will supply the one thing that most people will want to get away from in the twenty-first century, namely, a crowd. In the early 1990s world population was growing by 1.7 million a week. The current global estimate for

2025 is 8.6 billion. If the figure were to double every twenty-five years, a rate of increase currently observable in some parts of Africa and Asia, it has been calculated that there would be standing room only by the year 2330, because the total reached would be equivalent to the number of square yards on the surface of the earth.

Given the possible scenarios – nuclear war, plague, famine – that can be expected well before that point is reached, it may seem footling to speculate about the effect of population explosion on reading habits. But it is clear that, whatever the external disasters, people's attitudes to privacy and solitude are going to change – and that, of course, is where books come in. Reading admits you to an inner space which, though virtually boundless, is inaccessible to the multitudes milling around. This is likely to make it more precious and sought after as ordinary terrestrial space gets used up. At present the gap between people who read books and people who do not is the greatest of all cultural divisions, cutting across age, class and gender. Neither side understands the other. To non-readers, readers seem toffee-nosed. To readers, the puzzle is what non-readers fill their minds with. If in tomorrow's densely packed world reading becomes a lifeline to sanity for almost everyone, this gap will close – which will be a good thing for people as well as for books.

You might think that what people gain from reading hardly needs spelling out. But you would be wrong, because if it was obvious more people would read. In practice, explaining the point of reading to non-readers is extremely difficult. Also, it comes up against reasoned opposition. If you say that reading extends your mind, and allows you to lead more lives than one, non-readers will reply that those are just the advantages they gain from film and television. So what is special about reading?

What is special, oddly enough, is the result of an imperfection in the medium books use by comparison with the medium of film or television. Pictures of the sort relayed by film or television are an almost perfect medium, because they look like what they represent. Printed words do not. They are just black marks on paper. Before they can represent anything, they have to be deciphered by a skilled practitioner. Although accustomed readers do it instantaneously, translating printed words into mental images is an amazingly complex operation. It involves a kind of imaginative power different from anything required by other mental processes. If reading dies out, this power will disappear – and the results are incalculable. For reading and civilization have grown together, and we do not know whether one can survive without the other. The imaginative power reading uniquely demands is clearly linked, psychologically, with a capacity for individual judgement and with the ability to empathize with other people. Without reading, these faculties may atrophy. The translation of print into mental images also makes reading more creative than contact with other media, for no book or page is quite the same for any two readers. I do not mean by this that the reader is really the 'author' of the text – as it used to be fashionable for critical theorists to pretend – any more than a pianist playing Chopin is Chopin. But a reader, like a pianist, is engaged in an intense creative operation. If you are used to it, you will notice the effort it takes only when you leave off. Put your book aside and switch on the television and the sense of relaxation is instant. That is because a large part of your mind has stopped working. The pictures beam straight into your brain. No input from you is needed. What this means is that a democracy composed largely of television-watchers is mindless compared to a democracy composed largely of readers. Ours changed from the latter to the former in the second half of the twentieth century.

Because most people do not read books, reading is sometimes labelled élitist. But in fact it is no more élitist than walking – less so, because the government pays for you to learn to read, whereas you have to pick up walking by yourself. Nor are books just for the moneyed. You can get them free from public libraries. Some people are too lazy to read or walk but that has nothing to do with élitism. Admittedly, there are book snobs, and they do a lot of damage. They link reading in the public mind with swank and false refinement, and they frighten off would-be readers. That goes, too, for the lists of 'great books' concocted by panels of experts and published from time to time in the literary press. Who are these daunting league-tables meant for? Not, surely, other human beings. They seem more like end-of-term reports, dispatched to the Almighty, to show Him how well His earthly creatures are doing on the cultural side. Or maybe they are compiled on the model of the meritorious bric-à-brac that gets stuffed into space capsules – a complete set of US currency, a copy of the Geneva Convention, a diagram of the molecular structure of DNA – and blasted off towards remote galaxies in the hope of impressing extra-terrestrials.

The list I have put together is meant as an antidote to all that. Its contents are not chosen on grounds of literary 'greatness', the testimony they bear to the human spirit, or anything of that kind, though no doubt some would notch up reasonable scores even by those standards. Instead I took pure reading-pleasure as my criterion – the pleasure the books have given to me, and the pleasure I hope others will get from being reminded of them, or perhaps introduced to them. Aiming at a total of fifty, and sticking to the twentieth century, I started by jotting down the books I should most like to have time to re-read. That proved a bad plan. Half the available spaces were filled before I had got beyond the works of George Orwell, Thomas Mann, Evelyn Waugh and D. H. Lawrence. So I started again, allowing only one book per author. I also tried to choose a roughly equivalent number of books from each decade (though, as it turned out, I ended up with only one from the 1940s – humanity must have been otherwise occupied in those ten years). Since the criterion was pleasure, non-fiction was obviously just as admissible as fiction, and poetry as prose. The pleasure-principle also demanded that foreign books (in translation) should be allowed as well as English.

Without consciously deciding on it, I found myself avoiding the thumping masterpieces, and going instead for less trumpeted and less familiar favourites by the same authors (James Joyce's *Portrait*, not *Ulysses*; D. H. Lawrence's *Twilight in Italy*, not the novels; Aldous Huxley's *Those Barren Leaves*, not *Brave New World*). Books which I do not like, or have never been able to finish, were naturally omitted (no Proust, no Faulkner). It seems pointless to parrot other people's praise – indeed, worse than pointless. If you cry up unreadable books, just because they have been highly thought of in the past, you may deceive the young and innocent into trying them – and put them off reading for life.

I wondered, briefly, whether I ought to include books for their historical significance – reflecting the agonies and ecstasies of our catastrophic century. But that seems just another way of not trusting your own judgement. Books are not better for being about big events, often they are worse. The current vogue in university English departments is to reduce literature to politics – a way of engaging in the class war without actually risking income or lifestyle. In this context it is worth remembering Seamus Heaney's response to those who urged Northern Ireland's poets to say something about the troubles: 'In the end they will only be worth listening to if they are saying something about and to themselves.' This led me to omit books that gain their power from their subjects more than their writing (Kurt Vonnegut's account of the Dresden bombing, *Slaughterhouse Five*, for example).

A few books were reluctantly left out because they were too well known (Stella Gibbons's *Cold Comfort Farm*; Laurie Lee's *Cider with Rosie*). Admittedly there are well-known books left in, but they were the ones I could not resist. Books I agonized over but dropped included Nabokov's *Lolita*, T. F. Powys's grimly brilliant *Mr Weston's Good Wine*, Saul Bellow's *Seize the Day*, James Gould Cozzens's early disaster novel *S.S. San Pedro*, and Somerset Maugham's *Of Human Bondage*. Just typing out their titles sends me back to the list to try to squeeze them in. But none of the others seems willing to be squeezed out. So that is how it will have to stay.

Throughout, I have kept in mind H. G. Wells's Graham and the nightmare world he wakes up in. Besides being bookless, it is hideously overcrowded. Dense masses churn and roar everywhere. Graham breaks down under the stress, and begs tearfully to be taken to a little room where he can be alone. This scenario reflects Wells's gloom about population statistics. But it gave me an idea about which books to choose. Supposing Graham, cowering in his little room, with the deafening multitudes outside shaking the walls, finds, neglected in a corner, a dusty pile of books. He will discover, when he opens them, that they are from a century he did not live through (for he went into his trance in 1899). They will need to be really absorbing, to make him forget his ordeal. They will need to open a way to his own inner depths. They will need to make him laugh sometimes, and want to go on living. Above all, they will need to be appealing enough to enthral some of the semi-literate barbarians outside the door who, through his efforts, may start to reintroduce reading to a bookless world. It is a severe test, but I think these books pass it.

A. Conan Doyle
The Hound of the Baskervilles
~ 1902 ~

The Hound of the Baskervilles is not just a thriller. It is one of
the formative myths of the twentieth century. That may seem
a pretentious claim, and Sherlock Holmes would have cackled
with ironic laughter at the very idea. But it is true all the same.
It has achieved the status of myth because it has permeated
the culture at all levels, as myths do. Translated into every
major language, adapted for film, television and cartoon, it is
known to millions who have never heard of Conan Doyle.

It is no coincidence that as the nineteenth century ended,
writers started creating myths. Stevenson's *Dr Jekyll and Mr
Hyde* and H. G. Wells's *Time Machine* are other examples.
Universal elementary education, introduced in the 1870s, had
produced a huge new reading public, uncultured, but eager to
be entertained. Authors who rose to the challenge, Doyle
among them, needed a compelling style. But they also had to
identify and give fictional form to fears and desires deep in the
popular imagination. That is how myths are born, and it is
what *The Hound of the Baskervilles* does.

The dog of death, as John Fowles has pointed out, has the
longest pedigree of any canine species, recorded as far back as
Anubis, the jackal-headed undertaker god of ancient Egypt.

1

Folklore teems with black dogs that turn out to be the devil's minions. Dartmoor has its own version in the shape of the Wisht Hounds that hunt in the air as well as on earth and are led by Satan.

But Doyle's story of the Dartmoor hound is emphatically a twentieth-century myth because it rejects superstition. Holmes stands for reason and progress. He refuses to credit the legend of the spectral hound, and he is right. The hound does exist, and men run screaming to their deaths at the sight of it. But it is just a large dog daubed with phosphorus. Six rounds from Holmes's revolver put an end to it for ever. So much for the progeny of Anubis.

In the brave new world of Doyle's imagining, science replaces superstition. The new heir to Baskerville Hall announces that he is going to dispel the ancient gloom with electricity. 'You won't know it again with a thousand-candlepower Swan and Edison right here in front of the hall door.' Doyle's narrative has a comparable modern clarity, purged of hidden depths and arcane significances. If one of his highbrow contemporaries had written the story, the Grimpen Mire would have been stuffed with symbolism. It would represent femaleness or evil or the Freudian unconscious. In Doyle it is just a marsh – horrible, skinned with green sludge, a death trap to the ponies that sink screaming into its depths – but still just a marsh, not an excuse for pretentious abstractions that the reader is left to puzzle out.

The social order, too, is renovated. The novel spans England's past – from the prehistoric dwellings on Dartmoor to the seventeenth- and eighteenth-century portraits at Baskerville Hall. The aristocratic brutality of the Baskerville legend belongs to that past. But the new heir has farmed in Canada and lived in America. He brings with him the flavour of transatlantic democracy that, Doyle saw, would transform the world.

Despite these modern messages, Doyle wraps his story in mystery and menace as thick as the fog that envelops the moor at the story's end. As usual in his Holmes stories, the plot is less important than the setting. Not writing for a leisured readership, he has to create atmosphere with a few quick strokes – the granite tors, the fleshy-leaved bog plants, the blood-curdling cries that echo through the night. The result is unforgettably haunting, lingering in the mind long after you have forgotten the details of the action. So terror and superstition return, despite Holmes's bid to disperse them.

For that matter Holmes himself is really a magician, for all his appeal to reason and science. His feats of deduction are simply impossible. He identifies the manuscript of the Baskerville legend as early eighteenth century even before Dr Mortimer has taken it out of his pocket, and the evidence he gives for his dating – 'the alternative use of the long s and the short' – would hardly impress a paleographer. The Holmes stories are full of such miracles. Under the guise of science and reason, what they actually feed is our appetite for wonder. *The Hound of the Baskervilles* dramatizes our unsuccessful attempt to be rational, and nothing is more typically twentieth-century about it than that.

André Gide

The Immoralist

∼ 1902 ∼

This is a story about being true to yourself. Gide's hero Michel is a scholarly young man, carefully brought up by strict Protestant parents. He has already won acclaim as a classicist and ancient historian. To please his father he marries a childhood friend, Marceline, who is kind, beautiful and pious, but whom he does not love. On their honeymoon in north Africa, Michel's health breaks down. He coughs blood; a doctor warns him he is dangerously ill. Confronted with death, he realizes that he has never done what he really wants. Obedience to custom, culture and morality have stifled his true nature. He feels ashamed of his weak, pale body, and resolves to become healthy, bronzed and muscular, and to obey the promptings of his inner being.

As his strength returns, he discovers the life of the senses. The perfume of flowers at night sends him into raptures. He makes passionate love to Marceline – up to then their marriage had been unconsummated – but he is also powerfully drawn to the little Arab boys whom his wife pets and cares for. Their golden nudity excites him, and when one of them accidentally cuts his thumb, the glistening flow of blood seems like life itself compared with the slimy clots he coughed up during his illness. The boys he likes best are not the goody-goodies Marceline favours but the little thieves and scoundrels, because their budding criminality matches his own rejection of moral constraints.

When he and Marceline return to his ancestral estates in Normandy, his acknowledgement of his bisexuality becomes more open. He finds companions among the tough young peasants and farmhands. The academic studies that used to engross him seem dry and empty now. He is persuaded to give a course of lectures at the Collège de France, but devotes them to praise of the Goths who destroyed Roman civilization. Culture, he warns, is the enemy of life.

Though it was written in 1902, Gide's novel anticipates with remarkable accuracy the moral and sexual revolutions of the twentieth century. Michel's cult of the healthy body is accompanied by a Nietzschean contempt for the weak and for Christianity, which shocks Marceline, but which were to be prominent traits in Nazism. The hippie ethos of the sixties is prefigured, too, in Michel's rejection of conventional values. He develops a fellow-feeling with the poor and outcast, believing their life to be somehow more authentic than that of his own class. On a return trip to north Africa he sleeps out on the pavement with beggars. The children he loved on his first visit now disappoint him. Grown up, they have lost their childish beauty, and conform to social norms. 'How stupid honourable careers make people,' he thinks. He feels the typical dropout's disdain for normality. Most people, he believes, suffer from moral agoraphobia. However much they profess to want free-dom, they are terrified of being released from controls and restrictions. These were just the views that seemed so novel to the anti-Vietnam-war generation.

As he grows more dissolute, Michel's relationship with Marceline deteriorates. While he is spending the night with a male friend, she has a miscarriage. After that, she sickens. His remorse is mixed with disgust. For he will not submit to the virtuous hypocrisy of sympathizing with the diseased. In his eyes, her illness stains and spoils her. Out of consideration for her piety, he places her rosary in her hands as she lies dying. But she thrusts it away. Whether this means that she has been converted to his immoralist creed, or whether it is a rejection of him and anything he offers, we can only speculate.

In several respects, Michel's experiences mirror Gide's own. He too realized his homosexuality in north Africa in the 1890s, after marrying his cousin Madeleine Rondeaux. But his attitude to Michel is not simple. The story, he stressed, was neither an indictment nor an apology. Rather, it was an analy-sis of cultural trends. In his preface, he insists that Michel is not a special case, but exemplifies something of urgent general interest.

He compared the book to 'a fruit filled with bitter ashes', which might suggest that our – and his – disgust with Michel predominates in the end. But set against that is the captivating sensuousness of the writing. The African sunlight, like lumi-nous fluid, the sharp fragrance of lemon gardens at Ravello, the watery richness of apple orchards in Normandy – scenes like these submerge us in Michel's ardent life. Gide's achievement is to marry thought and feeling, so that we cannot be sure to which side of our natures to give preference.

Rudyard Kipling
Traffics and Discoveries
~ 1904 ~

The literati used to scorn Kipling for his imperialism. Nowadays they tend to admit that he was a genius, despite his regrettable attachment to the British Empire. But the truth is that his greatness and the Empire's were indivisible. It gave him his confidence, his imaginative exuberance, and his prodigious range of people and places. Imperial themes run through *Traffics and Discoveries*: patriotism, pride in the British Navy; outrage at the treachery of the Afrikaners in the Boer War.

But Kipling was no ordinary imperialist. He cared for the individual caught up in the system. His obsessive mimicry is a facet of this. The speakers in these stories include a Yankee gun-runner, a Sikh cavalry trooper, several British squaddies and naval personnel of various ranks, all pouring out their different brands of slang, jargon and technical know-how. The effect is to give each a distinctive presence, and that is crucial. Kipling's art reveals what is special even about seemingly nondescript people. The implications are democratic. Menials and underdogs in these stories repeatedly perform better than those in command. A boatload of misfits out-manoeuvres the top brass of the Channel Fleet. A humble Tommy vanquishes a young Boer toff, whose jeering voice reminds him of the squire back home. Kipling's estimate of the British army was 'brainy men languishing under an effete system'. That went for British society too.

'Wireless', one of the three masterpieces in this collection, is a weird tale that points up the uncommonness of the common man. It happens one freezing night in a chemist's shop on the south coast, where the owner's nephew has set up a Marconi apparatus and is trying to pick up signals from an associate in Poole. The chemist's assistant, on duty all night, is a downtrodden type called Shaynor who, it emerges, is dying of consumption and has a girlfriend called Fanny. The haughty nephew evidently despises them both. Gradually phrases and details accumulate that bring to mind Keats's poem 'The Eve of St Agnes'. The chemist's red, green and blue jars throw colours like the stained-glass window in the poem; a hare, like the hare in the poem, hangs outside a poulterer's shop. Shaynor goes into a sort of trance and begins, haltingly at first, to write out Keats's poem, as the astonished narrator peers over his shoulder. Questions put to him when he wakes elicit that he has never heard of Keats and does not read poetry. The narrator fumbles for a scientific explanation involving wireless waves. But the story reminds us that a downtrodden chemist's assistant with a girlfriend called Fanny was one of the world's greatest poets.

The second of this volume's classic stories, 'Mrs Bathurst', is also about the unexpected depths in seemingly ordinary people. Four men meet for a drink one blazing afternoon in a broken-down railway-truck beside a Cape Town beach. Among the circlings of their talk, they recall a young widow, Mrs Bathurst, who used to keep a hotel for sailors near Auckland. It turns out that a former shipmate of theirs called Vickery (nicknamed Click because of the noise his false teeth made) was fascinated by a 'biograph' picture – a precursor of the cinema – that showed her or someone very like her getting off a train in London. He has since disappeared. But a body has been found, its false teeth matching his, leaning against a tree in a teak plantation. The body has been struck by lightning and turned to charcoal. Another carbonized body crouches beside it. Is this Mrs Bathurst? What was the secret of their relationship? We never know. But the story's fearful end touches them with tragic grandeur.

The third of the masterpieces, 'They', is Kipling's tenderest story. Like 'Wireless' and 'Mrs Bathurst', it is about love. Deep in a Sussex woodland the narrator finds an idyllic manor house, presided over by a blind lady. Among the trees, children can be heard laughing and playing, but they do not allow themselves to be seen. Gradually we and the narrator realize that these are children who have died. He feels one of them kiss the palm of his hand – a secret sign – and knows it is his own lost child. Five years previously, Kipling's little daughter Josephine had died. Yet the story shuns sentimentality. The narrator decides that it would be wrong for him to visit the place again. It ends not with tears but with a stiff upper lip – the ethic upon which the British Empire was built.

Joseph Conrad
The Secret Agent
~ 1907 ~

Conrad hated revolutionaries, partly through guilt. In his native Poland he had been expected to take up the fight against Russian tyranny. Instead, he joined the British merchant marine and sailed the world's oceans for twenty years before becoming a writer. High-minded Poles denounced him as a renegade. In response, this novel presents political activists with corrosive scorn. It is one of the most exhilarating displays of irony in the language.

Unlike modern accounts of espionage, Conrad's is unglamorous. Mr Verloc, the secret agent, operates from a dingy Soho stationer's, specializing in soft porn. Fat, idle and self-righteous, he subsists by befriending foreign terrorists and betraying them to the authorities. His dupes are a grotesque bunch of central European freaks, pinned out on the page by Conrad's wit like biological specimens. But irony, in Conrad's hands, is not just destructive. Even Verloc retains a grubby kind of resilience, and the terrorists are sinister as well as comic. The most surreal is an explosives expert known as the Professor, who walks the streets with a bomb strapped to his body, and the detonator clutched inside his trouser pocket. The police, he knows, dare not arrest him, because he would blow them and himself to pieces. His dedication, though unfalteringly evil, is almost saintlike. He is pure and ascetic, treating himself on his rare holidays to a lonely glass of beer.

The Professor's opposite is Stevie, the idiot brother of Verloc's wife, Winnie. Stevie is kindness personified. Stories of injustice reduce him to whimpering rage. In one of the book's most cruelly funny scenes, he reprimands a cab-driver for whipping his horse, and is treated, in return, to a harangue on the miseries of cab-drivers. Unable to judge between horse and owner, and eager to make them both happy, he ends up wanting to take them both home to bed. Conrad believed that the universe was godless and uncaring, and through the half-witted Stevie he satirizes the fatuity of mere benevolence in such a setting.

Stevie's foolishness precipitates the book's climax. Verloc is under pressure from the (Tsarist) Russian secret service to organize what looks like a Communist bomb outrage in London, so that the British police will clamp down on leftist elements. He chooses Greenwich Observatory as the target and, to avoid unnecessary personal risk, gets Stevie to plant the bomb. Unfortunately Stevie trips, and is blown into such tiny fragments that the police have difficulty reassembling him.

At this point nemesis looms for Verloc in the shape of his wife. Conrad is often criticized for his insignificant women characters. But Winnie Verloc is capable of Shakespearean heights and depths. She has never loved Verloc, marrying him only to get a home for Stevie, to whom she is devoted. When she learns of his fate it almost deprives her of reason. Her final interview with her husband is one of the tensest scenes in literature. Verloc's emotional obtuseness is impregnable. He advises his wife to have a good cry and reminds her that things might have been worse. After all, he, rather than Stevie, might have been blown up. Meanwhile Winnie, half-mad with loathing, is desperately trying to blot out of her mind the phrases in the police report describing her brother's dismembered body. When Verloc tries to soothe her with a little marital foreplay, she seizes a knife and kills him.

Conrad said he chose an ironic method in *The Secret Agent* because it alone would enable him to say what he wanted in pity as well as in scorn. In the novel's final phase we see what he meant. The irony is drained of humour and becomes an austere and terrible truth-teller. Aghast at what she has done, Mrs Verloc imagines herself 'alone amongst a lot of strange gentlemen in silk hats' who are 'calmly proceeding about the business of hanging her by the neck'. Her apprehension of the jerk is so vivid that she seizes her head in both hands as if to save it from being torn off her shoulders. Panic-stricken, she flees to seek safety with the criminals and psychopaths who were her husband's former associates.

In the end *The Secret Agent* is not valuable for what it tells us about terrorism or murder – though it is instructive on both subjects – but for its style. Packed round with the ice of Conrad's irony, it is a supreme literary artefact. To re-read it is like playing a favourite CD. You listen not for plot or character but for the phrasing and cadences that give it its inimitable distinction.

E. M. Forster
A Room with a View
~ 1908 ~

This is Forster's happiest novel, and his most romantic. But it reflects serious beliefs that he never gave up. It works through a series of brilliantly lit scenes. You remember it as composed of sunlight and air. Early in the story Lucy Honeychurch, on holiday in Florence, and temporarily free from the clutches of her chaperone Miss Bartlett, buys some coloured prints of Italian art – Botticelli's *Birth of Venus*, Giorgione, Giotto. On her way back through the Piazza Signoria she passes two Italian men fighting. One is stabbed, and his blood spurts on to Lucy's prints. She faints, but George Emerson, a philosophical young railway clerk who happens to be passing, takes her in his arms and carries her to safety.

Nearly all the book's meanings could be extracted from this scene. The blood on the pictures – ordinary street-brawler's blood – reminds us that art is not the polite cultural commodity that Lucy's teachers and fellow tourists reduce it to. It is enmeshed in the body's desires, and is no respecter of persons. The pagan gods and goddesses in Lucy's pictures were, for Forster, real presences in the Italian countryside. His Italians pray to dryads just as eagerly as to saints. Phaeton and Persephone still walk the earth, in the form of a coachman the

14

tourists hire and a girl he picks up. For George and Lucy, engulfed in the Italian magic, the birth of Venus is no myth. As they embarrassedly sort themselves out after her fainting fit, they are already in the grip of love's divinity.

Pitted against them are priggishness, snobbery and custom, as represented by the other English guests at the Pensione Bertolini and their two attendant clergymen. The scenes of social comedy in which these guardians of propriety are anatomized are among Forster's sharpest. Though it advocates passion, the book radiates intelligence. Circumspectly, he distanced himself from vulgar simplifications of his subject by making one of the Pensione Bertolini ladies a novelist, who pens bodice-rippers about the steamy South.

He was eventually to give up writing novels because, as a homosexual, he was tired of pairing off boys and girls. But in *A Room with a View* he turns homosexuality to account by describing love through Lucy's eyes, not George's. She notices the shadows on his face, his body, his social awkwardness, and we notice them with her. How successful this is, women readers must judge. But for this male reader it is among the most sympathetic accounts of a woman falling in love that have been written by a man. Forster knew, too, about love crossing class boundaries. His most intense and lasting relationships were to be with lower-class men – an Egyptian tram conductor, an English police constable. The kind of middle-class fuss that Lucy has to contend with when she chooses George was familiar to him.

Lucy is not the only person who loves George. His father, old Mr Emerson, worships him – and this puts the love of one man for another at the novel's heart. For Mr Emerson is the truth-teller on whom the whole edifice rests. Outspoken, a little comic, very wise, he is the kind of character who might have come from a nineteenth-century Russian novel. But his ideas are militantly twentieth-century. A self-taught mechanic and Socialist pamphleteer, he is a crusading atheist. In Santa Croce he interrupts a lecturer who says that the church was built by faith to insist that it was built by under-paid workmen. Against Christian promises of an afterlife, he declares that we have come from the winds, and will return to them. All life is perhaps a brief blemish in the eternal nothingness. Yet he does not preach despair. He urges that, though we are ephemeral, we can say 'Yes' to life. We can follow our heart and brain, instead of joining the vast armies of the benighted who march to their destiny by catchwords.

Emerson has learnt this from his own heart and brain, not from reading. *A Room with a View* is a book that warns against books, or against too much trust in them. Cecil Vyse, the rich but bloodless aesthete whom Lucy abandons for George, lives for books, art and music. That is his defect. It leaves no time for people. 'People are more glorious,' cries Lucy, on the night she breaks off their engagement. It is a risky admission for a character from a book to make. But by this time Lucy is so real that we accept her as one of us.

G. K. Chesterton
The Man Who Was Thursday
~ 1908 ~

Chesterton subtitled this fantasy 'A Nightmare'. But that was a joke. It is one of the most optimistic books ever written and (a rare thing) combines optimism with brain-power. It fizzes with cleverness. You feel like applauding as you turn the pages, as if you were watching a conjurer. True, it resonates with robust Chestertonian Christianity as well, and that may put some readers off. But others will feel that if they did believe in a God it would be Chesterton's God they would choose.

The book's main target is moral relativism. The notion that right and wrong are just cultural conventions, not fixed and sacred values, seems modern to us. But it has been around for years, and Chesterton hated it. The late nineteenth-century philosophies that popularized it were, in his eyes, literally devilish. Philosophers (he makes one of his good characters in the book claim) are far more criminal than burglars or bigamists. Burglars respect property, they just want more of it for themselves, and bigamists respect marriage, otherwise they would not go through troublesome ceremonies to secure an extra share. But free-thinking philosophers cast doubt on the very ideas of property, marriage and family, and that makes them more dangerous than the most violent criminals.

Another highbrow belief that he detested was the idea that art ought to shock and upset people, and that artists are essentially lawless and rebellious. You might as well argue, he retorted, that it is artistic to throw a bomb in a crowded street. At the start of *The Man Who Was Thursday* that is precisely what is being argued by a posturing young anarchist poet, surrounded by a crowd of admiring women at a literary garden party. Opposing him with brilliant bursts of Chestertonian paradox is another young poet called Gabriel Syme, who maintains that the truly poetic subjects are law and order and respectability, and that the most poetical thing in the world is the underground railway.

Syme out-argues the snarling and baffled anarchist. But he has a tougher task in hand. For in reality, beneath his poetic disguise, he is one of Scotland Yard's new branch of philosophical detectives, pledged to eradicate dangerous trends in higher thought. His assignment is to infiltrate the General Council of European Anarchists, a septet of intellectual desperadoes whose codenames correspond to the days of the week. The President, Sunday, is a gigantic man, with an uncanny ability to read people's thoughts, and his confederates are all in various ways hideous and terrifying. One of them, Thursday, has just died, and the intrepid Syme, posing as a rabid anarchist, gets himself elected as Thursday's replacement.

His adventures in his new role are too thrilling to divulge, but they include a duel with an eerie, seemingly fleshless swordsman, and a series of desperate flights through the French countryside from armed police, peasants with axes, and a horde of mysterious black-clad troops. The monstrous Sunday is eventually cornered by Syme and his little bunch of lawmen, but he slips from their clutches and leads them on a wild chase, hijacking in rapid succession a hackney cab, a fire engine, an elephant from the zoo, and a hot-air balloon. Bizarre rhymes and jokes, scribbled on bits of paper, rain down on the bewildered pursuers. The last fantastic scene takes place at night in the grounds of a great country house. Torches and bonfires illuminate a carnival of dancers, all in elaborate fancy dress – disguised as windmills, lampposts, trees, wild birds. This phantasmagoria becomes the setting for a debate on one of the great Christian mysteries – why an all-wise, all-powerful God allows human suffering.

The quality that most shines out of the book is innocence. Chesterton could never have written it, you feel, if he had known the horrors that mankind was to perpetrate in the twentieth century, or even if he had seen eight years ahead to the Battle of the Somme. This is the last gasp of the golden Edwardian summer before Armageddon. It is a divine comedy by a man who still believes in valour, fair play, happiness and the triumph of good. Usually we feel superior to innocence, associating it with stupidity. But in Chesterton's case that will not work. If you think yourself cleverer than him, the odds are about ten million to one that you are wrong. So through these pages you can get back to a time when innocence, intelligence and hope went together. Not many books offer as much.

Arnold Bennett
The Old Wives' Tale
~ 1908 ~

When Arnold Bennett was living in Paris in 1903, he was dining one night in a restaurant on the Rue de Clichy when an old woman came in. She was fat and ugly, and carried a lot of small parcels which she kept dropping. The waitresses giggled. But to Bennett she seemed tragic. She must once, he thought, have been young and pretty, and she had aged by infinitesimal degrees, each unperceived by her. He resolved to write a novel about her, and that was the germ of *The Old Wives' Tale*.

In the event he wrote it about two women, Constance and Sophia Baines, the daughters of a linen-draper in the Potteries. When we first meet them in the 1860s they are sixteen and fifteen. Constance is obedient and conventional, Sophia wild and charming. Their lives are quite different. Constance stays at home to run the draper's shop, marries her father's assistant, Sam Povey, has a son, Cyril, and is widowed. Sophia elopes to Paris, is abandoned, but starts a small private hotel, and prospers. Despite their differing fortunes, the sisters are alike – thrifty, anxious, resolute. Bennett signals their similarity by artful parallels in their two stories, which switch about like musical themes. He learnt his technique from the French realists – Flaubert, Maupassant, Zola. But he adds a distinctive humour that is satirical but not belittling. The mark of a great novelist, he wrote, is Christ-like and all-embracing compassion.

For Bennett, however, compassion is not soggy. It involves understanding. The core of his writing is psychological truth, clinically observed, crisply reported. When the teenage sisters laugh at their slatternly char for having a lover, he records it as the 'profound, instinctive cruelty of youth'. His speciality is the generation gap, and the hostilities it breeds. The girls' father is an invalid, and must be nursed round the clock. But Sophia leaves him for a few moments to flirt with a salesman in the shop – and in that time he dies. Beneath all her grief and shame, she feels 'He did it on purpose'. The young devastate the old without a thought. Cyril wins a scholarship to art school in London, and hardly notices his mother's horror when he tells her. She foresees instantly that his going will kill her, yet 'She knew that she might as usefully have besought mercy from a tiger as from her good, industrious, dreamy son.' Many novelists go to their graves without writing a single sentence as fine as that.

The other psychological subject that absorbs Bennett is how important the small and the ordinary are to us. He was alerted to this when he came to write the section of the book on the Commune and the Siege of Paris. He was renting a house from an old French railwayman, and inquired whether his landlord had been through the siege. The old man turned to his wife and said, uncertainly, 'The Siege of Paris? Yes, we did, didn't we?' This made Bennett realize that to the mass of people the siege

21

was not the spectacular, thrilling event described in history. It hardly impinged on their everyday struggles. To Sophia the siege means only that she can sell her little stock of provisions at exorbitant prices, and has to pay a boy two sous an hour to stand in a food queue. Constance's life is composed of even more commonplace happenings – the birth of her son; the drama between her and Sam over whether she should lift the baby up when he cries; the terrible day when Cyril, aged nine, steals money from the till. But Bennett shows that such things are not commonplace, but vital. They are what we are made of. Sophia, with her little hotel in the Rue Lord Byron, has got used to the gas-lamp opposite being turned down at a particular time each night. It has become part of her life, dear to her. 'If it is possible to love such a phenomenon, she loved that phenomenon.'

Bennett's thoughtful redefinition of what love and importance mean would alone justify reading him. But from the viewpoint of the highbrows of his day he committed two unforgiveable sins. He came from the north of England and he made money by his writing. Bertrand Russell found him so vulgar he could not bear to be in the same room. The embargo has continued, and Bennett is almost entirely excluded from school and university syllabuses. It is bewildering and rather shameful.

H. G. Wells

The History of Mr Polly

$\sim$ 1910 $\sim$

Deep down, *The History of Mr Polly* is a novel of social protest, though it successfully disguises itself as something much jollier. Wells thought that English education was a scandal. He was fond of comparing the paltry outlay on schools with the massive government expenditure on armaments. Every battleship launched, he objected, stunted the lives of thousands of children. Alfred Polly is one of the stunted. A shopkeeper's son, he leaves school at fourteen, ignorant, confused, and with his natural curiosity almost stifled. Almost, but not quite. For beneath his vulgar exterior he has a sensitive soul and a romantic imagination. He loves long words, which he wildly mispronounces. Apprenticed to a draper, he chums up with two other culture-starved shop-assistants. They devour books – Shakespeare, Rabelais – and embark on glorious, ill-informed literary discussions.

None of this is a million miles from Wells's own life. The son of a shopkeeper and a domestic servant, he had to struggle to educate himself and was doomed to a career in drapery. He escaped by winning a scholarship to science college, whereas Mr Polly glimpses freedom when his father dies, leaving him a few hundred pounds. He buys a bicycle and explores the

Kentish countryside – a carless Eden of primrosed woods and dog-rosed hedges, where he finds romance. It bursts upon him in the shape of a red-haired teenager perched enticingly on the boundary wall of her private school. She tells him her name is Christabel and her people are in India. He feels like a knight in armour, and she gives him a tennis-blistered hand to kiss. Of course, nothing can come of it. Wells uses the scene to make us realize that Mr Polly's lack of education has blighted not just his job prospects and his chance of climbing the class ladder, but his access to a desirable mate as well.

Instead he marries his cousin Miriam, a spiritless ignoramus whose mother has her eye on Polly's nest-egg. Wells, too, married an unsuitable cousin early in his career. But he sloughed her off with the speed and efficiency natural to an upwardly mobile young genius. It takes Polly fifteen years. When we first meet him he is nearing forty and has a nagging wife, a virtually bankrupt draper's shop (bought with the remnant of his father's savings) and chronic indigestion. He resolves to burn the shop down and cut his throat, so that it will seem he died in the fire and Miriam will get the insurance money. The first part works wonderfully. Half the shopping district goes up in flames. But Polly is distracted from suicide by the realization that his neighbour's deaf mother-in-law is trapped on an upper floor. He rescues her and becomes a local hero.

The book might have ended there, with Polly reconciled to his lot. But, like Wells, he knows he is worth something better than the life in which fate has dumped him. He hungers for beauty, delight and repose. So he just clears out, tramps the country lanes, sleeps under hayricks, snuffs the scent of honeysuckle, and revels in the chirruping and cheeping in the woods. This brings him to the Potwell Inn, scene of his greatest ordeal. The Potwell Inn is a Wellsian idyll. Perched on the river bank, embowered in greenery, it is a favourite with trippers enticed by its beer and its beef and pickles. Its landlady is a paragon of plump good humour, who takes Polly on as odd-job man. Her granddaughter is a freckled charmer who reminds Polly of the girl on the wall. But there is a dragon in this paradise. He is called Uncle Jim, and is the landlady's nephew. He has been to a Reformatory, but has emerged unreformed. Periodically he descends on the inn, bringing terror, destruction and demands for cash. He has muscles of steel and smells dreadfully of spiritous liquor. Can Polly vanquish him and earn bliss?

The joy of the book is that under all its flippancy and bounce you feel Wells's sympathy for the waste and pathos of life. Even Miriam is redeemed. She ends up running a tea-shop bought with the fire insurance money. A childhood image that stays with Polly is of his father struggling to manoeuvre a sofa up the narrow back stairs of his shop. It comes to seem a symbol for the whole of troubled humanity, which wears itself out trying to get obdurate things round impossible corners. Polly, though, breaks free, and that is his lasting magic.

Maxim Gorky
My Childhood
~ 1913 ~

Gorky was five when his father died. He could not understand what all the fuss was about. His mother's grief repelled him. It made her look puffy and dishevelled, unlike her normal neat self. Standing by his father's open grave, he noticed some frogs at the bottom, two of which had managed to climb on to the coffin lid. When the gravediggers started shovelling in earth, they tried to climb up the sides, but the clods knocked them back. Afterwards their fate was very much on his mind, and he went around asking any adults who would listen whether the frogs had got out.

This glimpse of the child's alien viewpoint is typical of Gorky's book, and gives it humour and resilience despite the dreadful events it records. After the funeral, mother and son went to live with her parents in Nizhny Novgorod, where her father owned a small dyeworks. This was the beginning of the nightmare. The house was a seething bedlam of uncles, aunts, cousins and resident dyeworkers. Grandfather, a spry, polecat-faced old despot held sway, organizing ritual floggings for the children, and beating and kicking the women into submission. Gorky's uncles, brutal, vodka-sodden louts, would periodically go berserk and smash the house up. One of them had already beaten his wife to death. When sober they would sing maudlin love-songs to a guitar. Even the humour in the house was cruel. All the stories told were about people being tortured, ridiculed or persecuted. The foreman dyeworker was almost blind, and it was considered hilarious to heat the handles of his scissors red hot over a candle flame, and leave them for him to pick up. Gorky's mother remarried, but her husband, an army officer, soon proved as bestial as the rest of the family. When little Gorky first came upon him beating her, he seized a knife and tried to kill him, which earned the usual savage flogging.

Recalling the 'vile abominations' of that time, Gorky questioned whether it was wise to write about it. But he decided that he must, because until the poverty and squalor of Russian society were truthfully exposed they could not be rooted out. If we wonder why so many sensitive, intelligent young Russians supported the Revolution, despite its terrible human cost, Gorky's picture of life under the Tsars may help us to understand. He was to become a close friend of Stalin, and the presiding genius of modern Soviet literature.

But another reason why he decided to dredge up his childhood memories was that even in that loathsome world he found someone who sustained his faith in human goodness. This was his grandmother, an illiterate peasant woman, daughter of a crippled lacemaker. She had a soft, mysterious voice, so that when she spoke she seemed almost to sing her words, and they took root in the child's memory 'like flowers'. She could recite an enormous repertoire of stories about robbers, saints, wild animals, evil spirits and holy idiots. She believed that God sat on a hill on a diamond throne surrounded by silver lime-trees. She talked to Him familiarly, explaining everything that happened, and asking for His views. Once at early mass she had seen two angels, like patches of shining mist, helping the priest. She often saw devils, black and hairy, perched on the chimney-pots of people who were cooking meat during Lent. Even animals, she claimed, knew about God and felt shifty when they disobeyed Him. Her folk religion contrasted with her husband's strict orthodoxy. Each morning he would intone prayers before his treasured collection of icons, before launching on the day's brutalities. Grandmother's goodness did not save her from violence. When little Gorky first saw his grandfather punch her in the teeth, he felt sick with humiliation. But instead of getting angry or complaining she would try to explain to the child how grandfather's hard life and worries about money had made him the way he was.

Grandmother transforms the book. But so does Gorky's searingly accurate replication of a child's consciousness, seeing everything with glacial clarity, and annexing it to a hallucinatory interior world of poetic metaphor. The child's ardour for play and pleasure, in conditions that would demoralize an adult, is recalled too. Little Gorky learns to harness cockroaches to a paper sleigh with cotton threads. Along with the cruelties, he tucks away in his memory grandma's cream-

and-honey cakes and grandpa's dark-green vodka, distilled from cowslips and St John's wort. No book tells one more about childhood. All parents should read it.

Thomas Hardy
Satires of Circumstance
~ 1914 ~

One November morning in 1912 Thomas Hardy, alerted by a servant, went up to his wife Emma's bedroom and found her desperately ill. She could not speak, and died in a few minutes. Their marriage had been unhappy and Hardy was already involved in a relationship with Florence Dugdale, whom he soon married. But Emma's death prompted a series of poems, published in *Satires of Circumstance*, that have no match in English as articulations of bereavement. They are defiantly unconventional. Hardy had realized, much earlier than T. S. Eliot or Ezra Pound, that something drastic had to be done to drag English poetry into the twentieth century. He outlawed everything pretty and decorous. His language is an ugly mixture of dialect and coinage, parading a rag-bag of lexical monstrosities – 'chasmal', 'beneaped', 'fulth', 'brabbled' , 'darkled' – coupled with self-conscious modernisms – 'hydrosphere', 'wagonette'. Melodiousness is exiled too. It is replaced, in poems like 'The Going' or 'At Castle Boterel', by intricate metrical variations that control your reading as surely as a hand on your throat. The effect of all this technical daring is to make Hardy's mourning seem different and authentic, personalized by oddity.

The attitudes are odd, too. There is reproach in the poems. How could she have been so thoughtless as to die without warning?

> *Never to bid goodbye*
> *Or lip me the softest call.*

There is sardonic humour, as when a fashion-house catalogue arrives mailed to an addressee who has been for some months 'costumed in a shroud'. But most of all he remembers Emma as she was when he first loved her, in her 'air-blue gown', with her hair flapping her cheek as she rode beside 'the opal and the sapphire of that wandering western sea'. Stronger than grief or loneliness is his triumph in the supremacy of their love. Each moment together was worth the whole of eternity:

> *It filled but a minute. But was there ever*
> *A time of such quality, since or before?*

Compared to their shared and vanished love, the modern world is just 'urgent clack'. To feel like that about the modern world you do not, of course, need to be bereaved – only over forty and not stupid. Hardy's poems appeal to readers without his immediate cause for grief, because he speaks for the self-sufficiency of the individual soul, entrenched in its memories and values. That is what makes them heartening, despite their sadness.

Surrounding the poems about Emma are a medley of barbed, tough-minded poems about the disappointments of other people's lives. Many of these read like plot summaries of unwritten Hardy novels, and they deliver a narrative thrill missing from most modern poetry. 'There is the harvest of having written twenty novels first,' applauded Ezra Pound. Wives in these poems habitually deceive their husbands, sometimes fatally. A bridegroom overhears gossip about his bride in a public bar, and that night there is a splash by the harbour wall:

> They searched, and at the deepest place
> Found him with crabs upon his face.

Fishy horror eclipses hope in 'The Convergence of the Twain', too, where 'moon-eyed fishes' peer at the splendid furnishings of the *Titanic*. 'In the Cemetery' is a desolate poem about some mothers bickering over the exact position of their children's unmarked graves. We learn from the sexton that a main drain was recently laid across the site, so all the bodies have been moved and packed into a common pit. He refrains, however, from telling the mothers this:

> As well cry over a new-laid drain
> As anything else, to ease your pain.

Undignified, sour, unforgettable, that is typical of the secondary poems in this collection, and their cynicism creates a disturbing context for the poems that mourn Emma. Doubts and contradictions multiply. Hardy was an atheist, with no hope of human immortality. Yet these poems are crowded with ghosts, Emma's and others', who call to him, and whom he addresses as if they were alive. Are they just delusions? The poem 'A Plaint to Man' is ostensibly spoken by God, who asks:

> *Wherefore, O Man, did there come to you*
> *The unhappy need of creating me –*
> *A form like your own – for praying to?*

Is this an atheistic poem or not? It reduces God to an invention, but elevates him to a speaking presence. Uncertainties of this kind are integral to the book's power. So is the bitter humour of their presentation. Hardy surveys, with wry disenchantment, the unanswerability of all the big questions we want to ask.

James Joyce

A Portrait of the Artist as a Young Man

~ 1916 ~

Stephen Dedalus, hero of *A Portrait*, both is and is not the young James Joyce. But he is every child who has ever been bullied and terrorized, every adolescent who has ever burned with shame and sexual guilt. Joyce makes him a prig and an intellectual snob – like the young Joyce. But we do not feel superior to him, just as no father who is not terminally self-important can feel superior to his teenage son. For Stephen is alight with ardour and idealism, and even his vulnerability is a kind of strength, stemming from pure openness to experience.

How the mind works and how language works both interested Joyce, and he was among the first to suspect that the answers to the two questions might be the same. No novel of growing-up had used language so inventively before. It starts with baby Stephen learning the word 'moocow'. The sentences in this early part are relentlessly simple, as sense impressions and scraps of adult talk hit the child's alert receptors. With adolescence, the syntax complicates. Joyce's first version of the story had been verbose and circumstantial. Rewriting it for *A Portrait*, he reduced whole characters and incidents to unexplained echoes that flit through Stephen's thoughts. This fading-out of externals replicates the fathomless self-absorption of the young.

The title, like every word Joyce wrote, is precise. It is not a portrait of the artist as a young artist. To find art, Stephen must forsake religion, and he does as the story unfolds. The sadistic Jesuit masters at Clongowes College (Joyce's school as well as Stephen's) would be enough to cure most children of religion for life. But despite their repulsiveness they mesmerize Stephen, as they did Joyce. They exploit his innate purity. A hellfire sermon, preached in the school chapel, convulses him with horror, making him believe his commonplace masturbatory fantasies to be mortal sins. The priestly vocation appeals to his pride and loneliness. To merge himself in the common tide of humanity would be harder for this supercilious young man than fasting or prayer. Yet merge he must, Joyce wants us to understand, before he can become a true artist.

Stephen is saved from God by an epiphany. In Joyce's terminology epiphanies were commonplace events or objects that had a special, inexplicable radiance. He started recording them, as prose poems, when he was eighteen, and he works several into the text of *A Portrait*. He stole the term from Christianity (where it means the manifestation of Christ to the Magi) to signify that he was replacing religion with art. Stephen's epiphany happens when he is walking near Dublin harbour. He sees a girl standing in midstream, gazing out to sea. With her long slender bare legs and her skirts kilted up about her waist, she looks like a strange and beautiful seabird, and the white fringes of her underclothes are like a feathering of soft down. When she senses Stephen's gaze she returns it, without shame or provocation, gently stirring the water with her foot. We never discover who she is, nor does Stephen. But her face, 'touched with the wonder of mortal beauty', releases him from his priestly ambitions.

There is nothing more vivid or beautiful in all Joyce's writing. It has the clarity of truth – and was, indeed, true. It had happened to Joyce. Yet it is not just lifelike, but rich with myth and symbol. The girl rises from the sea like Venus, and she is like a bird because birds have special meaning for Stephen. Dedalus, in legend, was a bird-man; he made wings and flew. He also made the labyrinth, symbol of Joyce's cunning art, and he made a wooden cow (hence baby Stephen's 'moocow') in which Queen Pasiphae crouched to be mated by a bull.

These figures from myth are not invoked to diminish the human characters. On the contrary, they proclaim Joyce's belief that human passions are the same always and everywhere, and are what myths are made out of. Seemingly ordinary people like Stephen (or Bloom in *Ulysses*) have within them all the marvels of myth. 'In the particular', Joyce affirmed, 'is contained the universal.' Stephen, though a moneyless young man, rather averse to washing (as Joyce was), afflicted with body-lice and tormented by thoughts of women's underwear, is in the end right to see himself as 'a priest of the eternal imagination'.

D. H. Lawrence
Twilight in Italy
~ 1916 ~

We start in the snow. Lawrence is walking south through the Tyrol into Italy. It is September 1912. Around him the mountains are drifts and peaks of white. But here and there beside the path are crucifixes with wooden Christs hung on them, objects of veneration to the Bavarian peasants. For Lawrence this is not just a walking tour but an escape from the guilt and repression of the Christian north to the warmth of the pagan south. Six months before, he had met and fallen in love with Frieda Weekley, wife of his college professor. She had left England with him and was now tramping beside him through the snow. In his other accounts of the trek she figures vividly, but here he does not mention her. He presents his journey as a solitary one, a quest to find himself.

Unlike his novels, Lawrence's travel-writing exposes you to the full blast of his ego. You are swept up in his enthusiasms, and shown the world with the grime scrubbed off. He writes rapturously here about the sun and flowers – his two great loves. Taking lodgings in a village on Lake Garda, he lies in bed each morning watching the sunrise, from the first gash above the mountains to the molten flood filling his room. At sunset he watches the far mountain snows grow incandescent, 'like heaven breaking into blossom'. Outside, he finds English springtime flowers – primroses in nests of pale bloom, crocuses like lilac flames in the grass. For him the sun meant life – English winters would have killed him – and flowers symbolized not the frailty of beauty but its strength. He liked to think of their seasonal return outlasting the works of man. The pyramids, he said, would not last for a moment compared to the daisy. To be like a flower was his ideal – pure, unthinking, open to the sun. Few aims could have been less appropriate. For he was an intellectual to his fingertips, seething with ideas. The war between the thinking mind and the body's sensuous life filled him with rage and preoccupies his writing.

In this book he argues that they should be kept apart. As usual, he builds it into a theory. The Italian peasants, he decides, exemplify the physical, phallic consciousness that is essentially pagan. They are like tigers. Their god is Me. By contrast, the Christian north has made its God out of the Not-Me. It worships an idea, a remote deity. It cares for others and stifles the self. Intent on the Not-Me, it has invented science to explore the external world, and has discovered the machine. The horror, for Lawrence, is when the two kinds of consciousness come together. For then you have tigers armed with machines. By the time he finished writing his book, the First World War had begun, and tigers were killing each other with machines all over Europe.

Even before that, science and machines had defiled great tracts of the earth. Lawrence calls down curses on industrialism and its abominations. His answer in *Twilight in Italy* is to trust his feelings and instincts, not his mind. His prose is lulling, incantatory, and he loves or hates the people he meets with passionate arbitrariness. The Swiss, glimpsed on an Alpine hike, are the worst, he decides – soulless, materialistic, base. This is what Lawrence meant by letting the 'blood' think rather than the brain, and its dangers are obvious, especially in our post-holocaust age. But its counterpart was a tenderness towards the non-human that is erotic in its intensity. The moon above Lake Garda is 'like a woman glorying in her own loveliness'. She 'loiters superbly to the gaze of all the world', looking down at her 'quivering body, wholly naked in the water of the lake'. Shakespeare and Keats both shared Lawrence's passion for magicking things into people, and would have been proud to write that.

But the most haunting episode is his visit to the lemon gardens. The trees have been covered for the winter in great wooden sheds, raised on pillars. Heavy with pale fruit, they loom like ghosts in the underworld. The air is sweet with their blossoms, and along the dark paths are little orange trees, with dozens of oranges 'hanging like hot coals in the twilight'. To illustrate the essential Lawrence – sensuous, tender, vital – you could not better this passage. *Twilight in Italy*, though scarcely longer than a pamphlet, crystallizes his genius.

T. S. Eliot

Prufrock and Other Observations

~ 1917 ~

This slim volume by a young American bank-clerk working in Lloyd's Cornhill branch transformed English poetry. For originality, it put even Wordsworth and Coleridge's 1798 *Lyrical Ballads* in the shade. Most contemporary readers were baffled, and rightly. Bafflement was Eliot's plan. His problem was to reconnect poetry to the intellect rather than submerging it in the emotions as (he thought) the Victorians had done. His solution was to set the intellect impossible tasks. That way it would be permanently hooked, whereas possible tasks would have engaged it only till it had worked out how to perform them.

The three great poems in this booklet, 'The Love Song of J. Alfred Prufrock', 'Portrait of a Lady', and 'La Figlia che Piange' (The Girl who Weeps) are all strictly unintelligible, in that the information necessary for understanding them is withheld. Who are the 'you' and 'I' at the start of Prufrock ('Let us go then, you and I')? Are they Prufrock's two selves? Or Prufrock and the reader? Does he ever get to the room where the women:

> *come and go*
> *Talking of Michelangelo*

– and who are they? Who is the woman in 'Portrait'? What does she want of the young man? These and other unanswerable questions have generated so much paperwork from critics only because they have been mistaken for answerable questions, instead of being recognized as lures for the intellect. 'La Figlia che Piange' is the most baffling of all. The speaker seems to address a young woman in a garden ('Stand on the highest pavement of the stair . . . Weave, weave the sunlight in your hair') and to instruct her how to react to a man who has hurt her ('Clasp your flowers to you with a pained surprise'). But as the poem goes on it seems there is no man and no girl. The speaker has apparently just imagined them, or imagined their actions:

> So I would have had him leave,
> So I would have had her stand and grieve.

Eliot's friend John Hayward said that what inspired the poem was not a live girl but a grave-monument in an Italian museum. Maybe. Yet this is a poem about something other than a grave-monument.

The special power of all three poems is to impel you to understand and simultaneously stop you doing so. They unhook you from your normal connections with reality and leave you adrift in a region which is the more poignant because it is vague. But if they were just puzzles they would soon have died. What makes them live is Eliot's ear for poetic phrasing, which was his supreme gift. He did not have insight into human character compared to, say, Chaucer, or understanding of good and evil compared to Milton. But his evocative phrasing puts him on Parnassus with those great poets. His words seem to light up avenues in the brain that have never been opened before, but that we immediately recognize as the dwelling-place of our own feelings.

The result is ultimately just as emotional as the Victorian poets he tried to displace. In 'Prufrock', the feelings are of futility and self-deprecation:

> *I have measured out my life with coffee spoons . . .*
> *I should have been a pair of ragged claws*
> *Scuttling across the floors of silent seas.*

It is the sound as much as the sense that matters. The sense of the lines about ageing –

> *I grow old . . . I grow old . . .*
> *I shall wear the bottoms of my trousers rolled*

– is often missed. 'Rolled' trousers were trousers with turn-ups, considered rather sporty in Prufrock's day. But readers who imagine him as a shrunken oldster with rolled-up trousers find the hollow, echoing lines just as evocative as if they understood them.

'Portrait' is wittier. The young man, bewildered by his hostess's refined innuendoes, retaliates with silent jokes ('My smile falls heavily among the bric-à-brac'). But her martyred rejoinder as he takes off for a new life – 'I shall sit here serving

tea to friends' – incorporates the sadness of habit like Prufrock's coffee spoons, and (as with, say, 'Pray you undo this
button. Thank you, sir') shows a great poet making common
words unforgettable. Both these poems are matchless in their
way. Yet the third, 'La Figlia che Piange', seems to me the most
beautiful thing Eliot ever wrote. Its very indefiniteness makes
it heart-rending, like trying to remember lost love. Its figures,
real or imaginary, move like luminous ghosts in the sunlight.
It ends with a sudden orchestrated grandeur that is the more
moving because we do not know what there is to justify it:

> Sometimes these cogitations still amaze
> The troubled midnight and the noon's repose.

Edward Thomas

Collected Poems

~ 1936 ~

Edward Thomas had a wholly distinctive poetic voice. All poets must sound like themselves, not like someone else, if they are any good. But Thomas's voice is not only distinctive, it is also elusive, like a persistent, regretful note heard at the edge of hearing. In one poem he compares himself to an aspen tree that, shaken by the wind:

> *ceaselessly, unreasonably grieves,*
> *Or so men think who like a different tree.*

That downbeat last line is typical Thomas. His cadences stay with you for life, altering the way you feel. They are the sound of a mind accepting defeat, resigned, scrupulously honest.

He is thought of as a poet of the English countryside – the pre-tractor countryside of steaming plough-horses and bird-busy hedgerows. That was his poetic region, but he is a stranger poet than such labelling suggests. He was drawn to rain and weeds rather than pastoral landscapes. The noise of a storm – 'This roaring peace', he calls it – seems to have helped him forget himself. Weeds, particularly nettles, had the attraction of not being showy or hopeful – nearer to truth:

> *As well as any bloom upon a flower*

> *I like the dust on the nettles, never lost*
> *Except to prove the sweetness of a shower.*

Rain he valued not just for its beauty but for its discomfort, which was a kind of integrity. In one of his love poems the woman is 'Like the touch of rain' on flesh, hair and eyes.

There is no denying that he is a poet of Englishness, and this has earned him the contempt of intellectuals. But with him Englishness is not vulgar patriotism. It is a quest for something wild and unknown. He locates it in unpeopled places – thickets of hawthorn and hazel, too dense for a man to squeeze through, or the heart of a log-pile, where only the mouse and the wren can penetrate, or a dark and ancient hollow that is the badger's home, 'That most ancient Briton of English beasts'.

He writes about usual things – walking, gardening, chopping wood – with unusual depth. 'The Owl', one of his country-walk poems, contrasts his comfort at the day's end, safe at an inn, with an owl's cry, heard outside:

> *Speaking for all who lay under the stars,*
> *Soldiers and poor, unable to rejoice.*

'Sowing' (the best, I think, of all English gardening poems, just as 'A Cat' is the most truthful of cat poems) tells of a perfect day for sowing seeds. The soil is sweet and dry as tobacco dust. By nightfall all the seeds are in. Then, as every gardener hopes it will, comes the rain:

> *Windless and light,*
> *Half a kiss, half a tear.*

But the subject he returns to most often is his sense of something indecipherable. It is this that makes him a symbolist, writing intense but puzzling poems with an absence at their heart. In 'The Green Roads' the symbols are an old man, a child, goose feathers and a dead oak tree, but their meaning remains obscure. In 'The Path', children's feet have worn a path beside the road through the wood:

> *But the road is houseless, and leads to no school.*
> *To see a child is rare there.*

Wild birds and birdsong intrigue him – no one has written of them with more love and knowledge – and their appeal is partly that they are beyond understanding. The thrush sings 'an empty thingless name . . . a pure thrush word'. The poem 'She Dotes' is about a woman whose lover is dead and who tries to translate what the wild birds say. 'The Unknown Bird' is about a never-identified snatch of birdsong, heard in a beech-wood, 'As if a cock crowed past the edge of the world'.

This secret at the centre of things is sometimes threatening, 'An avenue, dark, nameless, without end'. That line is from 'Old Man', where he crumbles the grey leaves of the herb in his fingers, sniffing the bitter scent, and tries:

> *Once more to think what it is I am remembering,*
> *Always in vain.*

46

But sometimes, as in 'Lights Out', the dark avenue entices, promising rest:

> There is not any book
> Or face of dearest look
> That I would not turn from now
> To go into the unknown.

The war, and his impending departure for France, must have intensified this feeling, though depression and thoughts of suicide had long dogged him. He went into the unknown on 9 April 1917, when he was killed at Arras. But he left 144 poems that will not die.

Katherine Mansfield
The Garden Party
~ 1922 ~

Nearly half these stories are set in the New Zealand of Katherine Mansfield's childhood. There was a time when she had looked back on her prosperous, conventional life there with scorn. But two things had changed that. One was the loss of her beloved brother Leslie on the Western front in 1915. The other was her own approaching death. By the time she wrote these stories she was mortally ill with TB. But she wanted, before it was too late, 'to make our undiscovered country leap into the eyes of the Old World'. The first story, 'At the Bay', is a rhapsody of light, reliving scenes at the little seaside colony near Wellington where her family had moved when she was four. Its vitality sets the tone for the whole book. For though death intrudes in almost every story, melancholy is debarred. The focus is on those starting life, not ending it.

'The Voyage' is about a young girl, Fenella, going aboard a passenger boat with her grandmother. Her mother has recently died. But her own consciousness is bursting with life. Every sight and sound breaks over the child in a cataract of newness. This is typical of Mansfield's eager sympathy with youth. Leila in 'Her First Ball' spends the evening in a whirl of excitement, checked only when an elderly dancing partner talks about growing old, an impossibility that she sweeps incredulously out of her mind the moment he has gone. The central character in 'The Young Girl' teeters between being a sophisticated seventeen-year-old and wolfing cakes and ices with her little brother. Mansfield's darting technique omits the girl's name, along with all the other data a conventional story would supply. But every edgy word and gesture is scrupulously caught.

'The Daughters of the Late Colonel' is one of the funniest stories about death ever penned. Two terrified spinsters creep around the house after their father's demise, unable to believe the old tyrant has truly gone, and expecting him to jump out from cupboards and closets. Their temerity in arranging his funeral and actually having him buried horrifies them. What will he say when he finds out?

This is not just funny, of course. The women are victims of male power. Never allowed to use their minds, they now have none to use. Mansfield herself was wildly unconventional in her sexual couplings, and was alive to the traps that normal gender-assumptions set for women. But she is alive, in these stories, to the traps they set for men too. The husbands in 'An Ideal Family' and 'At the Bay' slave in offices to support their permanently holidaying womenfolk. William, a successful young lawyer in 'Marriage à la Mode', takes the train down from London to join his wife Isabel for the weekend. But she has invited a bevy of modern arty types, young poets and painters, effete and parasitic, whose prancing affectations

Mansfield satirizes. It is a story that her jealous contemporary Virginia Woolf could never have written, and it sees through everything Woolf stood for. As a 'colonial' and a banker's daughter Mansfield knew what it was to be cold-shouldered by the literati. 'Marriage à la Mode' is her answer. Isabel emerges as a worthless gull who betrays her hard-working husband in order to feel aesthetically in the swim.

The shallowness of literary people also pervades 'Life of Ma Parker', the saddest of these stories. Ma Parker chars for a writer who has followed his friends' advice to 'get a hag in once a week' to clean his flat. Vaguely aware that she has lost her grandson, he attempts condolence ('I hope the funeral went off all right'). Meanwhile the reader, inside Ma Parker's head, shares her memories of the child's beauty and tenderness and her speechless, aching grief.

The title story traces Mansfield's aversion to class-distinction to her New Zealand roots. The wealthy Sheridans (representing her own family) are giving a garden party when news arrives that a man from the nearby workmen's shacks has been thrown from his horse and killed. Mrs Sheridan has the grotesque idea of sending a basket of party leftovers – cream puffs, canapés – to comfort his widow and children, and young Laura (Mansfield's surrogate) is entrusted with this crass errand. In the event she is rendered speechless by the beauty and peace of the young man's body. '"Isn't life," she stammered. "Isn't life . . ." But what life was she couldn't explain.' Nor could Mansfield. But she could convey its wonder, and did.

Jaroslav Hašek
The Good Soldier Svejk
~ 1930 ~

Jaroslav Hašek was a comic genius in the flesh as well as in fiction. As editor of a magazine called *Animal World* in pre-First World War Prague, he livened it up by introducing formerly unnoted animals. His discovery of a fossilized flea caused a sensation, and when he advertised a pair of thoroughbred werewolves for sale the office was flooded with applications. He seems to have decided that the best way of dealing with a world full of fanatics was to agree with them as eagerly as possible, since opposition would only make them worse. When war came, he joined the Austrian army, got himself captured by the Russians, became an ardent Tsarist, and then, with the Bolshevik revolution, mutated into a commissar with the Red Army and editor of *Red Europe*.

A similar policy of non-resistance is adopted by his hero Svejk. When the novel starts in 1914 he has been discharged from the army for some years as a congenital idiot and is living peacefully in Prague attended by his charwoman, Mrs Muller. Her announcement that the Archduke Franz Ferdinand has been assassinated in Sarajevo in a car prompts a typical Svejkism: 'Well, there you have it, Mrs Muller, in a car. A gentleman like him can afford it.' Whether irony or stupidity predominates in such remarks is the question that soon perplexes the military authorities. For Svejk, re-entering the Austrian army with an alacrity rare among the Emperor's Czech subjects, finds himself confronting medical boards and courts of enquiry who earnestly enquire whether he is truly such a half-wit as he seems. 'Humbly report, sir, I am,' he invariably responds, beaming at them with his innocent blue eyes.

In encounters with superior officers he readily concurs with even their most insulting and bloodthirsty propositions. No one applauds pep-talks by the top brass more fervently. It would be glorious, he agrees, to be run through with a bayonet, and even grander to be blown to pieces by a shell. He is quick to reprove criticism of the army command, explaining, when confronted with some particularly gruesome military blunder, that 'Mistakes must occur'. His secret weapon is an enormous fund of irrelevant anecdote which reduces hearers, in extreme cases, to apoplexy and nervous breakdown.

Svejk's appointment as batman to a drunken and blasphemous regimental chaplain gives Hašek scope to satirize the Catholic church, which he detested almost as much as the Austro-Hungarian Empire. Svejk and his superior hold drumhead masses for the doomed troops, equipped with a folding field altar, on which the Son of God is depicted as a blithe young man 'with a handsome stomach, draped in something that looked like bathing drawers'. Another rich source of ridicule is official Austrian propaganda designed to inspire self-sacrifice in subject peoples. Placards depict feats of suicidal gallantry with cheerfully upbeat slogans. At railway stations ladies from the Society for the Reception of Heroes distribute boxes of mouthwash pastilles, inscribed 'For God and Fatherland', to battalions on their way to the front. A patriotic cadet in Svejk's regiment is engrossed in a treatise entitled 'Self-Education in Dying for the Emperor'.

There are gaps in the humour when Hašek lets us see the true atrocities. Manacled peasants, followed by carts bearing coffins, march to parade grounds to be shot for 'mutiny during call-up'. Photographs of executions carried out by the army in occupied territories show whole families strung up – children, mother and father – while soldiers with fixed bayonets guard the tree from which they hang. You might think it impossible, or indecent, to wring laughter from such situations. But that is the challenge Hašek faces with his blasts of sanity and scorn. Even a concentration camp is fair game. Svejk's charwoman Mrs Muller is arrested and court-martialled, but finding no evidence against her the authorities send her to a concentration camp, from which her family receive a card:

> *Dear Aninka, We are enjoying ourselves very much here. We are all well. The woman in the next bed to me has spotted —— and also there are here people with small ——. Otherwise everything is in order.*

Hašek started writing *The Good Soldier Svejk* in 1921, and had to publish the first volume at his own expense because publishers were frightened off by his obscenity and truth-telling. He was half-way through the fourth and final volume when he died in 1923. Though unfinished, his work has rightly been classed with the comic epics of Cervantes and Rabelais and is funnier and more fearful than either. His message was that war is not merely cruel, unjust and obscene but ludicrous. Unfortunately humans are programmed to believe otherwise.

Aldous Huxley
Those Barren Leaves
∼ 1925 ∼

Novelists do not come cleverer than Aldous Huxley – nor, for
that matter, do human beings – and this is one of his cleverest
novels. It is set in Mrs Aldwinkle's sunny palazzo overlooking
the Tyrrhenian Sea, where a party of English guests are enjoy-
ing the late summer. They talk brilliantly and paradoxically
about everything that interested bright young people in the
1920s: art, books, politics, whether Freud is bogus, how Rela-
tivity has changed science. They also make love. Lord Hoven-
den, disciple of the Socialist Mr Falx, persuades the delectable
Irene, Mrs Aldwinkle's niece, to marry him by driving round
and round Lake Trasimene in his Vauxhall Velox, until she
gives in. Mr Calamy, ex-guards officer, beds the young novelist Mary Thriplow.

Beneath this sparkling surface, however, an anti-novel gradually accumulates, challenging the house-party's airy chat.
Calamy, as he makes love to Mary, considers how it gratifies
his love of power to have her shuddering with pleasure in his
arms, 'like one who has been tormented on the rack'. With a
man, he thinks, he would vent his need for power by making
him suffer, but with a woman he does it by making her enjoy.
This self-awareness chimes with Huxley's consciousness of

the parasitical nature of the society he describes. To sustain Mrs Aldwinkle's cultural refinements (Mr Falx muses) men and women labour in Peruvian guano beds, in Australian freezer-trains packed with mutton, in the heat and dark of Yorkshire coal-mines. Huxley belonged to the Aldwinkle class (she was based on Lady Ottoline Morrell), and his feelings of social guilt help to explain why he described this novel's theme as despairing scepticism.

Not that it seems despairing. Most of the time he depends on comedy to make his point. Francis Chelifer (a poet and editor of the *Rabbit Fanciers' Gazette* who joins Mrs Aldwinkle's guests) has invented a game to take the tedium out of office work. It brings, he boasts, all the thrills of the fairground – the big dipper, the roller-coaster – right to your desk. All you have to do is pause for a moment in your daily grind and ask yourself: Why am I doing this? What is it all for? Where will it end? Ask yourself these questions thoughtfully enough, recommends Chelifer, and, firmly seated though you may be on your office chair, you will feel that the void has opened beneath you, and that you are sliding, faster and faster, into nothingness.

The terror of death most afflicts Mr Cardan, a ruthless, age-ing hedonist, who persuades a half-witted young heiress to marry him. Before they can wed she dies horribly of food poi-soning. She reminds him, in her agonies, of a favourite cat he once had, a beautiful grey Angora, that was fatally addicted to eating black beetles, and died vomiting shreds of her shard-torn stomach. Cardan feels sorrier about the cat than about the moribund half-wit, and the whole episode is icily unsentimental in typical 1920s mode. But it steers the novel inevitably towards religious questions.

Some cope with these better than others. Mary Thriplow settles down anxiously to think about God – a spirit, she tells herself, an infinite emptiness. She pictures a vast expanse of sand beneath a huge dome of sky. But just as she is getting into the right mood, three camels appear from nowhere on the edge of the picture and lollop along absurdly, ruining her meditation.

Later, in bed, Calamy lectures her about the nature of reality, taking his own hand as an example. To a physicist, he explains, his hand is a mass of atoms, each with negative electrons whirling round a positive nucleus; to a chemist, it is a collection of complicated molecules; to a biologist, a set of specially programmed cells. But it is also part of a moral being, capable of good and evil. It has written thousands of words; it has killed a man, it has touched her body – 'He laid his hand on her breast; she started.' This speech is the crux of the novel and, in a sense, of Huxley's career. More and more after this he forsook his early cynicism and asked himself what the connection was between Calamy's different worlds – between consciousness and chemistry, between electrical charges and good and evil. The search took him into mysticism, and into hallucinogenic drugs as a mystical pathway. He did not find the answer. But nor, yet, have we.

F. Scott Fitzgerald
The Great Gatsby
~ 1925 ~

Everyone agrees that *The Great Gatsby* is a classic, perhaps the supreme American novel. But its spell is hard to account for. Its key symbol is a rubbish tip. Fitzgerald borrowed this idea from the dust heaps in Dickens's *Our Mutual Friend*, but his tip is more fantastic – a valley of desolation, where 'ashes grow like wheat into ridges and hills and grotesque gardens'. Over this wasteland loom two huge eyes on an optician's billboard, like the eyes of a dead god. The novel's catastrophe takes place here, and all the characters continually pass by it, driving between Manhattan and the millionaires' houses with their private beaches on the north shore of Long Island.

Whether the valley of ashes accurately represents American life as Fitzgerald depicts it is the big question. Everything in the book is like a prism. As you turn it, it reflects different lights. The hero Jay Gatsby is young, handsome and fabulously rich. Celebrities flock to his parties, where men and girls come and go 'like moths among the whisperings and the champagne and the stars'. His past is dazzling. Oxford-educated, he lived like a young rajah in all the capitals of Europe, hunted big game, collected rubies, and, when the war came, led his machine-gun battalion with daredevil gallantry in the Argonne forest. Afterwards, the insignia of three German divisions were found among the piles of dead.

Most, if not all, of this is false. Even Gatsby's name is a lie. Born James Gatz, of poor North Dakota farming folk, he was adopted, aged fifteen, by a shady businessman, and worked on his yacht in some vague personal capacity. After war service, he went to Oxford for five months as part of a demob scheme. In league with bootleggers and gangsters, he has made his fortune from illicit alcohol and stolen bonds. His mansion with its Marie Antoinette music-rooms and Restoration salons is pure kitsch. His parties are inane, drunken orgies. The famous guests do not even know their host.

So is the rubbish tip a fitting symbol for Gatsby? Yes and no. Though a pathological liar, he is an idealist, gripped by an 'incorruptible dream'. When he was a newly commissioned officer, before he went to France, he fell in love with a girl of good family, Daisy Fay. She was the first 'nice' girl he had known. By the time he returned, she had married Tom Buchanan, a man of impeccable social credentials and enormous inherited wealth. But Gatsby still worships her. He has fabricated his extravagant lifestyle solely to impress her. He has bought his mansion because it is across the bay from Tom and Daisy's, and at night he gazes, trembling with passion, at the lights of her house.

We can see, as Gatsby cannot, that Daisy is worthless – empty, spoiled, cowardly. What he sees, and adores, is her effortless grace. She gleams like silver, safe and proud above the hot struggles of the poor. 'Her voice is full of money,' he murmurs wonderingly to Nick Carraway, the narrator. So even his incorruptible dream is corrupt, a compound of snobbishness and dollars. Or so a strict moralist would say. But Fitzgerald makes us want to defend Gatsby against moralists. The contrast with Tom Buchanan is crucial. For Tom – womanizer, prig, racist – is entirely hateful. We watch him casually break his mistress's nose as a punishment for getting above herself. We watch him denounce Gatsby, in front of Daisy, as a common swindler, and sneer at his pink suit and his affected Anglicism ('Old sport'). The more he goes on, the more Gatsby and his dream win our sympathy.

Fitzgerald said that the burden of his novel was 'the loss of those illusions that give such colour to the world that you don't care whether things are true or false as long as they partake of the magical glory'. For Gatsby, Daisy partakes of magical glory, and he never loses that illusion. He dies tragically and, in a way, heroically, since he saves her. She is not worth saving, of course. But perhaps everything we cherish is illusory in the end – a valley of ashes. It is our faith in illusions that gives life value. Fitzgerald's plangent poetry seems to be saying that – but it is impossible to be sure. His tight little plot, simple as a Greek tragedy, radiates doubts like artificial rainbows around a fountain. That is why we read it again and again.

Mikhail Bulgakov

A Country Doctor's Notebook

~ 1925–7 ~

In 1916 Mikhail Bulgakov qualified as a doctor at the university of Kiev. He was twenty-four and, with the ink scarcely dry on his diploma, he was despatched to the wilds of north-west Russia to take charge of a small regional hospital. It was midwinter, there was no telephone, roads were impassable. But from the snowbound countryside there came daily a macabre procession of ailing peasants, walking-wounded or carried on sleighs, for him to cure. These stories, each as keen and bright as a scalpel, are the record of how he coped.

Told in a callous way, the material would be unbearable. But Bulgakov's frankness and self-deprecating humour make it deeply appealing. His youthful appearance is a dreadful worry to him, especially when he notices the kindly but critical glances of the two midwives who are his assistants. He tries to talk in a deeper voice, and move more slowly, as befits a real doctor. Alone at night, he breaks into cold sweats at the thought of the cases that may arrive next morning. A strangulated hernia? Peritonitis? From the delivery room and the operating theatre he rushes across the yard to his study, and frantically tries to make some connection between the complicated diagrams in his anatomy textbooks and the helpless human beings patiently waiting for him to save them.

An urban creature, he hates the countryside and the loneliness. The nearest street lamp, he bitterly calculates, is thirty-two miles away – and the nearest cinema. Yet to us as readers the life he describes seems exciting and fulfilling. His study, with its green-shaded kerosene lamp and its gently humming samovar, becomes a familiar, cosy haven, from which we sally forth in Bulgakov's company to do battle with death. Answering a call for help from a colleague twenty miles away, he is driven through a blizzard in a horse-drawn sleigh, keeping a pursuing pack of wolves at bay with his automatic pistol. The casualties that arrive at his hospital are scarcely less hair-raising. A young woman who has had her leg torn off in a flax-crushing machine; a child dying of diptherial croup, whose throat he has to cut open to insert a silver pipe so that she can breathe. In the course of this operation his technician faints, almost tearing the child's windpipe out as he falls. Yet both patients recover and turn up a few months later in his consulting room glowing with health and gratitude. The reader is allowed to feel, by proxy, the responsibility, the expert concentration, the triumph, that in reality only a skilled surgeon can feel.

His success with these cases is gossiped about, magnified, hailed as miraculous, and the stream of patients becomes a flood. He works far into the night in the operating theatre, drags himself to bed, plunges, pole-axed, into sleep, only to be hauled back to consciousness by a battering on the outer door announcing some nocturnal emergency. Rifling through his records at the end of his first year he finds that he has treated 15,613 patients. His feelings about the peasants in his care are a mixture of idealism and exasperation. Their stupidity beggars belief. Issued with a fortnight's supply of a drug, carefully measured out in daily doses, they swallow the whole lot at once and have to be stomach-pumped back to life. Syphilis is rife among them, passed on from adults to children. Yet when he warns them, in the early stages, how the disease will progress, they eye him with grinning disbelief, and refuse the irksome treatments he recommends. The night, the blizzards, that lie beyond the glow of his green-shaded lamp, become a symbol for a deeper darkness – the medieval ignorance of the Russian people – that weighs on him as on many young intellectuals of his day.

Meanwhile, far away at the battlefront, a new world is being born. The last story in this collection is about another young doctor, hiding in Kiev, listening excitedly to the guns of the approaching Bolsheviks. Arrested and dragged before the brutal White Russian cavalry commander, whose atrocities have spread terror through the town, he survives by a prodigious feat of daring. Contrasted with him is the central figure in the previous story, Bulgakov's successor in the remote regional hospital, who, overcome by loneliness, became a morphine addict and shot himself. Both stories, in different ways, celebrate courage – the virtue that shines from every angle of this profoundly human collection by the greatest of modern Russian writers.

Sylvia Townsend Warner
Mr Fortune's Maggot
~ 1927 ~

In 1918, when Sylvia Townsend Warner first moved to London, she was too poor to join a book club, so she signed on at Westbourne Grove public library. One book she borrowed was a volume of letters by a woman missionary in Polynesia, which pleased her because it had the minimum of religion and a lot of everyday life. It must have stayed in her mind, for one morning in 1925 she woke up remembering a very vivid dream. A man stood alone on an ocean beach, wringing his hands in despair. She knew that he was a missionary, and that he was on an island where he had made only one convert, and that at the moment she saw him he had just realized that the convert was not a convert at all. She jumped out of bed and began to write it down, and that was the beginning of *Mr Fortune's Maggot*.

'Maggot', she explains at the start of chapter one, is an old word meaning 'A whimsical or perverse fancy'. Her missionary is the Revd Timothy Fortune, who works for many years in the Hornsey branch of Lloyd's bank, until an inheritance from his godmother allows him to train for the ministry. Why he chooses to go to the South Seas is not clear. Perhaps that is his maggot. On the remote island of Fanua he is the only white man. The natives are charming and childlike, always singing and dancing, and they are delighted with Mr Fortune, who brings with him many intriguing novelties, including a second-hand harmonium and a silver teapot. They have no word for chastity, and Mr Fortune is mobbed by bevies of giggling, naked maidens inviting him to come swimming.

His attempts to gain converts to Christianity are politely ignored, except in one case. A naked brown boy called Lueli comes and kneels beside him the first time he celebrates matins, and joins him in his lonely hut as pupil and acolyte. Their love is the subject of the novel. It was a delicate topic to handle in 1925. Writing it, Warner said, was like being pregnant with a Venetian glass child. She presents the relationship as innocent. There are times, especially in fits of anger, when Mr Fortune longs to throw Lueli to the ground and ravish him, but his inhibitions are far too strong, and beyond an occasional fatherly kiss there is no erotic contact. Mediated through Warner's wit and intelligence, it seems a much more probable scenario than our current moral panic about paedophilia would lead us to believe.

In the event it is Mr Fortune, not Lueli, who is seduced – or educated – by the island. Its lushness bewitches him. It is an earthly paradise, where the ripe fruits fall from the trees and the air is sleepy with salt and honey. Gradually, under its sway, his rigid soul blossoms. He spends hours in blissful idleness, watching the clouds. His body is rescued from years of neglect and repression. After initial stern refusal, he allows Lueli to massage him with fragrant coconut oil (he tells himself, in extenuation, that it is really a manly, athletic rub, like Elliman's Embrocation). As he unwinds, his faith in the Christian God vanishes, and he comes to see that to impose Him on the islanders would be like turning rifles and gunboats against their bows and arrows. One day he finds that Lueli, despite his lip-service to Christian doctrine, actually worships a small garland-bedecked idol that he keeps in a grove of flowering trees. The disclosure fills him with rage and horror at first, and it is only after the idol has been destroyed, and Lueli has almost died mourning for it, that he understands the folly of his obstinate Christian righteousness.

His decision to leave the island follows. For he sees that in trying to change and educate Lueli he has been killing the thing he loves. Lueli will be Lueli only if he remains remote, intact, incalculable. Mr Fortune's love can outwit its inherent urge to meddle and destroy only by renunciation. So he sails away, broken-hearted.

Warner pursues the psychology of the story with beautiful accuracy, and seems to have felt distress at where it led her. She added a postscript: 'My poor Timothy, good-by! I do not know what will become of you.' Three years later, she began her long, tempestuous but deeply happy lesbian relationship with Valentine Ackland. So, unlike Mr Fortune, she found an alternative to renunciation.

Evelyn Waugh
Decline and Fall
~1928~

Those who think of Evelyn Waugh as a venomous old snob should try the early novels, written when he was still vulnerable and adrift. His basic problem was low self-esteem. At Oxford he worshipped the poseurs and popinjays from the smarter colleges and felt inferior because he was just a suburban publisher's son, without wealth or title. Undersized and pug-faced, he tagged along behind the Bright Young People, getting drunk at their parties, and wallowing in remorse afterwards.

His first novel, *Decline and Fall*, makes fun of all this, and of himself. Refreshingly defiant, it satirizes the aristocrats and those who kow-tow to them, not least the sickening creeps who ran Oxford in the 1920s. Paul Pennyfeather, the likeable hero, is assaulted by a mob of drunken undergraduates and, with breathtaking injustice, sent down as punishment, because the dons dare not discipline the upper-class hooligans who were the real culprits. This was not very like Waugh's own inglorious departure from Oxford with a third-class degree. But it had the advantage, as revisionist autobiography, of substituting innocent victimhood for mere failure, and since Waugh had been led astray by moneyed wastrels he might justifiably claim to be a casualty of the class system, like Paul.

Unfit for any career, Paul gets a job teaching at a prep school in north Wales, just as Waugh had done, and the misfits he meets are all, in various ways, comic reflections of Waugh. The butler Philbrick, who spins exotic lies about his past fame and grandeur, parodies Waugh's shame at his respectable home background. The irrepressibly indecent Captain Grimes turns Waugh's anxiety about homosexuality into farce. Waugh regretted his homoerotic romps, and destroyed his 'quite incredibly depraved' Oxford diaries. Grimes, however, learns to accept his sexual nature with far less fuss, passing from prep school to prep school, seducing pupils *en route*. Only when forced into heterosexuality does he panic. Obliged to marry the headmaster's daughter, he leaves his clothes and a suicide note on the beach, and is duly mourned – though actually he survives, just like the young Waugh, who attempted suicide by swimming out to sea, but turned back on meeting a shoal of jellyfish.

Meanwhile the third assistant master, the Revd Prendergast, gives a comic spin to Waugh's real-life religious worries. Two years after *Decline and Fall*, he was received into the Catholic Church. But for some time before that he had been torn between faith and doubt, and so is the delightfully absurd Prendergast, who (though none of the other oddities of Christian doctrine trouble him) cannot fathom why God should have made the world.

Given Waugh's general opinion of mankind, he might well have found this puzzling too. But in this novel the level of human warmth is unusually high – if, that is, we exclude the aristocrats, particularly the female ones, who range from the terrifying Lady Circumference ('Sorry if we're late. Circumference ran over a fool of a boy') to the beguiling Margot Beste-Chetwynde, to whom Paul becomes engaged. Margot's enormous fortune is partly derived from the white-slave trade, and she makes it appear that innocent Paul is her accomplice. When the police swoop, he gets seven years' penal servitude, whereas she escapes scot-free. This contretemps obliges Paul (and Waugh) to confront his infatuation with the aristocracy. He decides that he will not give Margot away to the authorities, much as she deserves it, because she belongs to a higher species than himself. It is right, he muses, that there should be one law for common mortals, and another for her. This was roughly the young Waugh's position when sucking up to the toffs at Oxford. But seeing it spelt out by Paul, we recognize its fatuity.

Besides, the rationalist Professor Otto Silenus, one of Waugh's happiest creations, is at hand to put Paul right. When he burbles about Margot's uniqueness, the Professor corrects him. Compared with other women of her age, he observes, the differences are infinitesimal – a few millimetres here and there. Such variations are inevitable in any species, but in all her essential functions – her digestion, for example – she conforms to type. It is a wholesome lesson for anyone who finds himself hopelessly in love, and perhaps it is how Waugh, hopelessly in love at the time with Olivia Plunket Greene, tried to comfort himself. Like much else in this novel, it comes from the deep, cool well of intelligence that he discovered within himself and that he had, to date, singularly failed to draw on in real life.

Robert Graves
Goodbye to All That
~ 1929 ~

In 1929 Robert Graves left England for Majorca under the
spell of the young American poet Laura Riding, abandoning
his wife and four children. This autobiography was written by
way of excuse. He seems to have felt that if he exposed the
callousness and stupidity of the English class system, which
he had suffered from since childhood, readers would not
blame him for clearing out. Complaint did not come easily.
His English upbringing had taught him to hide his feelings.
One of the fascinations of the book is how it contrives to sound
self-confident while cataloguing disaster.

Things went wrong for him early on. He was half-German
(his mother was related to the great historian Leopold von
Ranke) and to his schoolfellows this seemed socially unaccept-
able. At Charterhouse he was bullied so persistently that he
came close to nervous breakdown. It convinced him that the
public-school spirit was 'a fundamental evil', which you could
eradicate only by dismissing staff and pupils and tearing down
the buildings. When he joined the second battalion of the Royal
Welch Fusiliers on the western front, he found it steeped in the
same snobbery and prejudice. New officers were referred to as
'warts' by their seniors, and routinely humiliated. Despite the

war situation, petty rules abounded. In the mess, only captains or above were allowed to drink whisky or turn on the gramophone. Subalterns had to attend riding lessons every afternoon. Minor dress regulations were enforced with bone-headed obduracy. When the mauled remnants of the battalion limped back to their trenches after the Battle of Loos, the colonel sent a message to say that he had noticed some men with their shoulder straps unbuttoned and trusted it would not happen again.

But the book never dwindles into complaint. Graves was young, proud and complex, and had internalized many of the social codes he condemned. His response to the bullying at Charterhouse had been to learn to box and win both middle- and welterweight cups – scarcely a renunciation of the public-school spirit. The Royal Welch's battle honours and regimental traditions filled him with boyish enthusiasm. He came to agree with the blimps that smartness on parade was vitally linked with morale in combat. Though he professed to regard the war as a wicked folly, he despised pacifists. When his brother officer Siegfried Sassoon published a pacifist manifesto, it was Graves who talked him out of it and persuaded him to get medical help. These contradictions ran right through his life – maverick and martinet were always tangling inside him. Far from damaging the book, the clash gives it human credibility. A complete personality emerges.

His war-reporting, too, seems unedited, mixing the grotesque and the banal. An impromptu, behind-the-lines cricket match uses, as wicket, a large cage containing a dead parrot.

Hungrily stripping the currant bushes in an overgrown garden one afternoon, he comes on his Company Sergeant Major at the same task, and they both slink away embarrassed. Events like these preserve the human scale amid the carnage. So does Graves's studiously calm manner, which brings an air of polite surprise to the direst situations ('I had never seen human brains before; I had somehow regarded them as a poetical figment'). His divided nature betrays itself in vacillation about killing. Sniping from a knoll in the support lines, he sees, through his telescopic sight, a German soldier taking a bath. To shoot a naked man seems distasteful, so he does not fire. However, he hands the rifle to his sergeant, who does.

Early in the Somme offensive he was officially killed himself. A shell splinter hit him in the back and exited through his chest. His colonel wrote telling his mother of his death, and it was announced in *The Times*. Meanwhile Graves lay in a corner of the dressing station and 'amused' himself watching bubbles of blood escape through the opening of his wound. The pretence at sang froid is typical. In fact he was shattered by the war. It took him years to recover. Shells would burst on his bed at night; ghosts accosted him in the street.

His book has become history. More English readers, probably, know about the Great War from it than from any other single source. But it is history with the inconsistencies intact: history before the historians have smoothed it out. Though it is an anti-war book, it displays just those qualities – courage, pride, patriotism – that make war happen.

William Empson
Seven Types of Ambiguity
~1930~

In 1929 a fourth-year undergraduate at Magdalene College, Cambridge, read an essay to his tutor about ambiguity in a Shakespeare sonnet. Impressed, the tutor suggested he should pursue the subject, and the next week the undergraduate turned up with a 30,000 word typescript. The tutor was I. A. Richards, the student William Empson, and the typescript was the core of *Seven Types of Ambiguity*, a book that revolutionized the study of literature in the English-speaking world. Later that summer Empson won a starred first in English and a research fellowship. Shortly afterwards, however, a college servant found a packet of contraceptives in his rooms, and he was banished from the university for ever. He wrote up *Seven Types* for publication back home in Yorkshire, while trying to re-plan his life.

The breezy, unacademic style, combined with an intelligence obviously far in advance of that of most academics, is one of the book's great attractions. The project, he explains, grew out of his thinking about pieces of poetry that seemed to him to be beautiful, but without his knowing why. He tried to account for his feelings by teasing out all the different meanings the words had for him, and in this way he turned each poem into an expanding cloud of possible ambiguities. 'Ambiguity' he defines as any verbal nuance, however slight, that gives room for alternative reactions to the same piece of language. He came to the conclusion that all good poetry was ambiguous in this way – that ambiguity was, indeed, the defining quality that made poetry poetic.

He was a matchlessly sensitive and ingenious reader, and watching him at work on one of his favourite examples (Macbeth's 'Light thickens, and the crow/Makes wing to the rooky wood', say, or 'Bare, ruined choirs, where late the sweet birds sang' from Shakespeare's Sonnet 73) is like being in a dark room when someone switches on the light. Just as brilliant and dramatic is the language Empson himself finds to describe the effects of ambiguity. Othello's strangely vague use of the word 'cause', before he kills Desdemona ('It is the cause; it is the cause, my soul'), is diagnosed as a mind 'baffled by its own agonies'. The jewels and perfumes on the dressing table in T. S. Eliot's *The Waste Land* 'blur the grammar into luxury'.

The examples of ambiguity are selected from the whole historical spectrum, starting with Chaucer, to show that English poetry has always been ambiguous. Other European languages, being more tightly bound by grammatical rules (gender in nouns, distinctive verb endings), lack this potential, Empson suggests – which may explain the relatively high count of great poets in English.

The division of his subject into seven types is, he admits, just a convenience. Ambiguities are themselves ambiguous, and cannot be pigeon-holed. But the book gradually advances from cases where the ambiguity merely modifies the apparent meaning to cases where the two are diametrically opposed. Some of these are complex, but some are quite simple, like Jonson's 'Drink to me only with thine eyes' where the last two lines of the first stanza ('But might I of Jove's nectar sup,/I would not change for thine') say the opposite of what they are supposed to. Thinking about opposites takes Empson to the heart of his subject. Language and cognition, he points out, depend on binary oppositions (up, down; young, old) where each term implies, but also denies, its contrary. In ambiguous poetry (and, he notes, in Freudian dream analysis) opposites converge, and this is what allows poetry to strike deeper than the superficial clarities we impose on everyday life.

A consequence of Empson's thesis is that readers, when they read poems, really make them up in their own minds. Eliot had said that this was the mark of the bad critic. But Empson insists it is inevitable. The reader constructs the vital cloud of ambiguities, and some readers are better at it than others. It follows that there is no question of a final reading. Poems are not fixed or definite, but always being reread differently. The critic's job is not to extract what is 'really there', but, Empson maintains, to create the taste of his period. Virtually all the developments of continental and American literary theory in the later twentieth century sprang from these premises. Mostly they were developments that Empson heartily deplored. But he had let the genie out of the bottle.

W. B. Yeats
Collected Poems

~ 1933 ~

For some poets, human life is enough. It was for Shakespeare, most of the time. Others – Dante, Milton – can grow to full stature only if they voyage beyond life into heavens, hells and mythical shadowlands. W. B. Yeats belongs among these. He seems to have been born tired of the earth. In one of his earliest poems he laments the dullness of modern life and its lack of visionary ardour:

> *Of old the world on dreaming fed,*
> *Grey Truth is now her painted toy.*

Science and democracy had done the damage, he believed. Between them they had killed off the supernatural presences that mankind once walked among, and had dethroned the valiant aristocrats who, he liked to think, had held sway in the golden age. Against the new idols of the market-place, he proclaimed the exclusive value of poetry: 'Words alone are certain good'. Against fact and materialism, he asserted the supremacy of the imagination:

> *There is no truth,*
> *Saving in thine own heart.*

These are proud boasts, and a small poet would look ridiculous making them. Fortunately Yeats was not small. He wrote like God. He could put words together with such certainty that they seem to have been graven on tablets of stone from the beginning of time:

> Things fall apart; the centre cannot hold;
> Mere anarchy is loosed upon the world,

or:

> Man is in love, and loves what vanishes,
> What more is there to say?

Like nearly all his great poetical statements, these disparage earthly life. Yet they do not come across as disparagement. Their grandeur exalts them. They turn loss into beauty. Like tragic drama, they give humankind something to fling in the face of suffering and death.

Yeats is often thought of as an escapist. But it is his pain, and his ability to communicate it, that justifies the escapism. It is because he can write:

> She was more beautiful than thy first love,
> And now lies under boards,

that we do not think him whimsical when he heads off towards wonderland. His escape-routes often lie through interstellar space, where free spirits, who have sloughed off the flesh, play among the wandering stars. As time went on, he accumulated a bizarre panoply of creeds that could liberate him from the prison of common sense – Rosicrucianism, reincarnation, cyclical patterns of history based on the phases of the moon. Some of these came to him, he believed, direct from the spirit world, via Mrs Yeats's automatic writing. They seem ludicrous until you look at the poetry they made possible. Without the history-cycle nonsense we should not have 'The Magi':

The uncontrollable mystery on the bestial floor,

or 'The Second Coming':

What rough beast, its hour come round at last,
Slouches towards Bethlehem to be born?

or 'Leda and the Swan':

A shudder in the loins engenders there
The broken wall, the burning roof and tower,
And Agamemnon dead.

Why one of our supreme poetic masters should have needed the help of beliefs that would disgrace a fairground fortune-teller is a question that takes us to the heart of the modern poet's predicament. Dante and Milton did not have to worry. Their readers still believed in other worlds. Yeats, born into a secular age, had to make up his own religion out of whatever scraps came to hand. What mattered was not its truth but its wonder, its ability to make the real world seem dowdy and unreal.

From the start his poetry had sought this, often in the

magical women of Irish folk-tale – the girl for whose sake wandering Aengus vows to:

> pluck till time and times are done
> The silver apples of the moon,
> The golden apples of the sun,

or the woman in 'The Secret Rose', with hair of such shining loveliness,

> That men threshed corn at midnight by a tress,
> A little stolen tress.

As Yeats aged, his thirst for wonder grew. His heart still felt young:

> sick with desire,
> And fastened to a dying animal.

He longed to get out of his body and become an artificial golden bird, singing to the lords and ladies of Byzantium, and scorning,

> In glory of changeless metal
> Common bird or petal.

It is, you might say, a ridiculous ambition. But its senselessness is what frees it. His poetry is like music – not because it sounds beautiful, though it does, but because it conquers rationality. Listening to a Beethoven symphony, you do not ask 'Does it make sense?' because you know it has got beyond that. So with Yeats.

Christopher Isherwood
Mr Norris Changes Trains
~1935~

A month after *Mr Norris Changes Trains* was published, Hitler introduced conscription in Germany, and it became clear to all but the most optimistic that war was on its way. Many of the book's first readers must have turned its pages with fascinated dread, seeking clues to the coming terror. Isherwood had lived in Berlin from 1929 to 1933. He had witnessed the sporadic civil war between Communists and Nazis, culminating in Hitler's appointment as Chancellor in January 1933 and the start of the Nazi anti-Jewish campaign. In the novel these events come across in vivid flashes of reporting – bullet-slashed posters on hoardings, knives whipped out in street-corner brawls, the corpses of rival martyrs paraded for newspaper photographs, well-heeled Berliners at café tables glancing approvingly at uniformed Nazis striding past.

The central figure of the novel, Arthur Norris, remains fastidiously aloof from these messy goings-on. We first meet him on the train to Berlin, sharing a compartment with the narrator, a young Englishman called William Bradshaw. Mr Norris is a gentleman of the old school. Bradshaw notices at once his beautifully manicured hands and his luxurious wig – held in place, Mr Norris later confides, with a dab of glue. His conversation is a fusillade of arch giggles and nervous tics. In his elegant Berlin flat, a male secretary and a manservant cushion him from life's rougher edges. He enjoys a wide acquaintance in the capital. Through him Bradshaw meets Olga, a procuress and cocaine dealer, and Anni, a prostitute specializing in corporal punishment, of which Mr Norris is a delighted amateur. At the other end of the social spectrum they get to know Baron von Pregnitz, a closet homosexual with a monocle and chronic Anglophilia ('I find this so very nice, your English self-control, you see'). Surprisingly, Mr Norris is also on friendly terms with Ludwig Bayer, the city's leading Communist. Social injustice, he twitters, when William quizzes him about his leftist sympathies, offends his sense of the beautiful. He has hated it ever since he was once unfairly punished by his nurse.

Mr Norris's charm and sympathy are sometimes a little overdone. 'Dear, dear, nature is really very cruel,' he murmurs, when William's landlady's canary dies. But there is nothing else to warn William – or us – that he is not perfectly harmless; nothing except his eyes, which are pale blue jellies with no human spark. It is only at the novel's end that William discovers the truth. He first hears about the casualties from a journalist friend, after returning to England. Von Pregnitz, surrounded by the police, shot himself in a public lavatory. Ludwig Bayer's body was spotted by other arrested Communists at the police headquarters, with one ear torn off. Mr Norris betrayed them both. He lived by blackmail, espionage and treachery. His thuggish secretary, of whom he always pretended to be in mortal dread, was his obedient Mephistopheles, and the two have escaped together to South America to continue their predatory operations.

The novel's terse, colloquial prose was a spin-off from writing for film. Isherwood had spent the previous summer working on a screenplay for Gaumont-British, and it did wonders for his style. Where Mr Norris came from is more of a question. He is usually identified with Gerald Hamilton, a colourful character who ran the Berlin office of *The Times*, and had once helped steal a Greek millionaire's wife's jewel-case from the Blue Train. There are certainly similarities. But it seems probable that Isherwood also constructed Mr Norris out of parts of himself. He went to Berlin at a stage in his life when he was contemptuously dismissive of conventional morality, and cynical about political causes ('All politicians are equally nasty'). In both respects he resembled Mr Norris. Further, what attracted him to the city, as he frankly admitted, were the boy-bars where hungry youngsters would sell themselves to foreign homosexuals for the price of a meal. However much he might suppress it, it can hardly have escaped someone of Isherwood's intelligence and upbringing that this was blatantly exploitative (and would have been equally so, of course, had the prostitutes been girls, not boys). He was using the misfortunes of the stricken city as an opportunity for his own hedonism, just like Mr Norris. Maybe Isherwood's personal involvement with the character explains why Mr Norris is so insidious. He prompts the thought that the face of evil is not monstrous or diabolic, but weak, self-seeking and a bit pathetic – not so very unlike our own.

Elizabeth Bowen
The House in Paris
~1935~

The contents of this novel, generally reckoned Elizabeth Bowen's best, are passion, betrayal and violent death. But what you are most aware of as you read is intelligence. It suffuses everything, like a delicate but powerful solvent. No writer has ever pursued people's thoughts and feelings – or half-formed thoughts and half-recognized feelings – with such keen intricacy. She is unusually alert to how the senses and the mind interact. Early in the novel the main character, Karen, visits her uncle and aunt. Her uncle, while rooting daisies out of the lawn, breaks the news that his wife must go into hospital for an operation. 'A hurt earthy smell rose from the piteous roots of the daisies.' Despite its mundane setting, that sentence would not be out of place in a world of dryads and wood-gods, creatures that cross the barrier between humanity and external nature that Bowen persistently dissolves. Her characters keep reading their feelings into objects – the 'sad stare' of an orphanage, the 'unkind white height' of a ship at leave-taking.

This sensitivity transforms her writing about sexual relations, where body and mind are in heightened states of intensity. She is fascinated by gender difference. The novel starts with two children meeting each other for the first time at a house in Paris. Henrietta, aged eleven, is using up a few hours between train-connections. She is on her way south to stay with her grandmother, a friend of the house's owner, Mme Fisher. Leopold, aged nine, is there to meet his mother, also known to Mme Fisher, whom he has never seen, or not that he can remember. Unsmiling, intelligent, wary as little animals, the two act out, when left alone together, the male and female sleights and subterfuges that will be taken up by adults later in the book. Their talk, like much in the novel, is alive with hidden meanings. Henrietta has a toy monkey called Charles, and when Mme Fisher's grown-up daughter Naomi asks her if she still plays with it, the child replies, 'I like to think he enjoys things.' You can read that either as fantasy, or as a precociously adult admission of self-deceit ('I like pretending he enjoys things, but of course he does not'). In the second sense it exposes the egotistical face of altruism. We want the warm glow of imagining that other people are happy, even when we know that, like Charles, they cannot be. The bleak potential of Henrietta's seemingly innocent remark spreads across the novel, touching almost all its relationships.

The middle section, called 'The Past', takes place ten years before the children meet, and recounts a brief love-affair between Karen and Max, an ironic intellectual who has intrigued her ever since she was a teenager. Hopeless and joyless, it is less like a love-affair than the placating of an angry need. But for the reader the settings give it its special feel – a garden with a spectacular flowering cherry, a restaurant in

Boulogne, a rain-sodden night in Hythe. These are show-pieces of Bowen's internalized scenery. They become what the lovers are made out of, expressing the tempo and pressure of their passion, so that we understand Max when he says that only images and desire exist.

And time too, of course. Karen's uncle, the lawn-weeder, is also a clock-fanatic: 'each room vibrated with a metallic titter'. Time shadows the novel. Its burden is the passing genera-tions. Upstairs in the Paris house, Mme Fisher lies dying. She completes the triptych of which the children and the lovers are the first two leaves. What is happening to her body now is too terrible to acknowledge, so she resorts to malice and laughter. The novel's disasters, we gradually learn, are mostly her do-ing – which means that it is her tragedy too.

Yet the result is far from melancholy: Bowen's intelligence sees to that. Her dialogues are not realistic, but compounded of terse, brainy rhetoric like an intellectual game. She keeps producing sentences that you want to learn by heart to help you understand life better. It is true that she could not write as she does if she had not read Henry James first. But she goes beyond her mentor. She is James plus sex. Besides, James was male, by and large, whereas Bowen is female to her finger-nails, and knows things men do not. Perhaps that is why men tend not to read her. It is also why they should.

John Steinbeck
Of Mice and Men
~1937~

George and Lennie are itinerant farm workers in 1930s Cali-
fornia. George is small and quick. But Lennie is gigantic, with
superhuman strength and the brain of a half-witted child.
Why they stick together puzzles everyone – or, rather, why
George sticks with Lennie. Lennie sticking with George is no
mystery. He worships him, imitates his gestures, and hangs on
his every word. Maybe it is George's good nature that ties him
to Lennie, feeding him, chivvying him, trekking with him
from job to job. Or maybe Lennie's earning power is the draw.
For George dreams of saving up enough to buy a smallholding
for the two of them and settle down in ease and plenty. His
account of this idyll, its phrases polished like a treasured fairy-
tale, is Lennie's greatest treat. He is always begging George to
repeat it, though he knows it by heart. There will be a little
house with a fat iron stove, and pigs and chickens and a cow, and
the cream will be so thick you'll have to cut it out with a knife,
and – this is Lennie's favourite bit – there'll be a hutch of rabbits and it will be Lennie's job to feed them with pickings from
the alfalfa patch. The rabbits appeal to Lennie because he is a
gentle giant, or means to be. He likes stroking soft and delicate
things – mice, puppies, women. The result is invariably disas-

trous. The mice and puppies become small crushed corpses, to Lennie's pained surprise. The women bawl for help, and George and Lennie find themselves hiding in irrigation ditches while a lynch-mob scours the countryside for them.

At the start of Steinbeck's story, this tragic Laurel and Hardy arrive at a new farm, where their reputation has not preceded them. The other workers are friendly. The boss seems decent. But Curley, the boss's son, is a problem. He is small and pugnacious and hates big people like Lennie. Worse, he has recently married and his wife is a shameless trollop, always hanging around the men's quarters and chatting them up. She likes the look of Lennie. With these fateful figures in place, the story builds to its knuckle-whitening climax. The tension is almost unbearable, and is achieved without comment from Steinbeck. You can imagine how a Victorian writer would have milked the situation – George's goodness, Lennie's childish innocence – like the misty-eyed double act of Amy and big, dumb Maggie in Dickens's *Little Dorrit*. But here sentimentality is outlawed. The effect is entirely modern. No century but ours could have produced a narrative so bare, so relentless. It is as near to perfection as a work of art can be. It is also a democratic text. Though it has the emotional peaks and precipices of grand opera, the diction is simple, the dialogue ordinary farmhand argot.

The story's meaning is a grim one for stories. For what destroys George and Lennie is a story, or a dream that has turned into a story, as dreams do. If only they had been like animals, not thinking beyond the present, not imagining a brighter future, they would have been safe. But human beings are different from animals because they have a dream, as Steinbeck shows. The other farm workers who overhear George reciting his idyll all want to come along too and take a share in the smallholding. His is not, it turns out, a special, personal dream, but the fantasy of every loser. What is more, Curley's wife, the fatal Delila of the plot, has her dream too. Though coarse and stupid, she imagines she is cut out for a job in the movies. She met a film actor once who told her she had talent. Her destiny is with the stars. These are the lies, Steinbeck seems to be saying, that ruin us. But these lies make stories, and stories make us human, and a story is what Steinbeck is telling.

The undreaming, un-story-telling animals are always there in the background. On the first page, before George and Lennie stumble in, we see the tracks of deer and racoons on a little sunny patch by the Salinas river. At the end, by the same stretch of river, a water snake glides through the shallows, and a heron's beak lances down and swallows it. Man with his passions and hopes is a temporary misfit, Steinbeck seems to imply, in this factual, ruthless, beautiful world.

Graham Greene
Brighton Rock
~ 1938 ~

Brighton Rock is a novel that got out of hand. The indications
are that Greene meant it to be quite a different book from the
one he wrote. He had been reading T. S. Eliot's *The Waste Land*,
and he set out to echo the poem's indictment of soulless modern culture. The opening description of Brighton on a Bank
Holiday Monday foregrounds just those features of the twentieth century – popular newspapers, advertisements, fun-loving
crowds – that intellectuals like Eliot lamented. Fifty thousand
trippers cram into the town. Excursion trains from Victoria
unload at five-minute intervals their unappetizing cargo of
clerks and common, spotty girls. Eliot's distaste for mechanical modern life (the typist in *The Waste Land* with her 'automatic hand') is sedulously reproduced too. The novel features
a disabled car-park attendant, moving his leg with a mecha-
nism worked from his pocket.

But as Greene's creative juices began to flow, this snobbish
gloom lifted. He was, in real life, keen on Brighton – and it
shows. The fresh and glittering air, the women in beach pyja-
mas, the slot machines on the pier, the Victorian pubs, the
hotel terraces sprouting bright umbrellas – the whole panorama
fans out like a carnival, and for the first time (his previous

novels had been comparative duds) we watch the distinctive Greene effect that processes tat and squalor into aesthetic riches.

It was in its characterization, though, that the novel really rebelled against its author. The two main characters are Pinkie and Ida. Pinkie is a seventeen-year-old double-killer, at the head of a razor gang who run a protection racket up on the racecourse. He is as pure as ice – never touches alcohol, is nauseated by women and sex. Ida is a big, blowsy thirty-something, always game for a bit of fun, partial to oysters and Guinness and cheap pathos. But the crucial difference between them is that Pinkie is a Catholic, whereas Ida's interest in religion stretches no further than her ouija board.

When he wrote the novel, Greene had been a Catholic for ten years. At Balliol he had fallen for a young Catholic woman who would not marry him unless he joined her Church. So he did. There were problems. He had difficulty believing in God. But he found the idea of Hell attractively unsentimental, and liked annoying friends by boasting that only Catholics were capable of spiritual reality. Everyone else was invincibly ignorant. In *Brighton Rock* he turned this provocative claim into fiction, creating his own genre of spiritual thriller. The thesis of the book is that Pinkie (and the pathetically stupid sixteen-year-old Rose, who is infatuated with him) are superior to Ida simply because they are Catholics. They live in the true realm of good and evil, whereas she inhabits the trivial shadowland of right and wrong. Pinkie is implicitly compared to Christ; Ida is a picture of vulgar fleshliness – 'cow-like' eyes, big breasts, port-winy laugh.

But the more Greene heaps insults on Ida, the more the novel turns against him. She takes on the role of detective, uncovering truth, adamant that justice should be done. When the police are baffled, she works out how Pinkie's first victim died and she hunts Pinkie down, saving Rose, whom he plans to murder. Her name, which she shares with a Greek goddess, relates her to a pre-Christian world. She comes to represent implacable, archaic motherhood, protective, punitive, eclipsing the male – and she outshines Pinkie as a human being in every respect.

Pinkie, too, refuses to become the character his creator planned. Greene later told an interviewer that he had tried, as an intellectual exercise, to invent a being whom the reader would accept as worthy of hell. But that is not how Pinkie turns out. As the novel develops, we learn that he is a victim of poverty and deprivation. Reared in a cramped slum, forced, lying alone in the dark, to listen to his parent's love-making every Saturday night, he has grown up twisted. Mocked and defeated by the big-time gang-boss Colleoni, cold-shouldered, in his cheap suit, by waiters and hotel-receptionists, he seems more and more just a posturing child, whom no reader, much less the Christian God, could condemn to eternal fire. So the novel was saved by its characters from Greene's intentions. It became his first masterpiece – thrilling, spectacular, alive – pitting the insane pretensions of religion against humanity's common sense.

A. E. Housman
Collected Poems

~1939~

Death is everywhere in Housman's poems. In that respect they are very like life. In other respects they are less so. He invents a simplified pastoral world, ostensibly sited in rural Shropshire, but in fact as far from any recognizable reality as Willow-pattern Land. But by blurring time and place he makes his setting universal. He deals in elemental passions, stripped of period dress.

His message, too, is universal. Crudely paraphrased, what the poems say is what any self-respecting, buttoned-up male might say when asked how he is: 'Mustn't grumble.' But beneath this stoical restraint there is another voice in the poems that grieves, curses and begs for pity. The double-act is, again, entirely lifelike. 'Mustn't grumble' always carries a subtext of grumbling. It is a way of scoring points for courage while asking for sympathy. Housman gives this common human subterfuge the dignity of great art. There are poems that advise proud silence, on the grounds that 'Horror and scorn and hate and fear and indignation' would be futile in a world of inescapable cruelty. And there are poems 'Sick with hatred, sick with pain'.

There are also poems where the two stances mix.

> *The toil of all that be*
> > *Helps not the primal fault;*
> *It rains into the sea,*
> > *And still the sea is salt.*

You cannot tell from those lines whose the 'primal fault' is. It may be man's original sin. Or it may be death, the flaw in creation foisted on mankind by 'Whatever brute and blackguard made the world'. Read one way, the lines counsel resignation. Read another, they cry out against universal injustice. The poems constantly balance on this ridge between stoicism and outrage. In one of the most moving ('Tell me not here, it needs not saying'), the poet remembers the ecstasy he has felt in communion with nature. But he knows that when he is dead, and some other person walks the same paths:

> *heartless, witless nature,*
> > *Will neither care nor know*
> *What stranger's feet may find the meadow*
> > *And trespass there and go.*

You can read 'heartless, witless' literally, and conclude that this is a poet who understands that nature is not an animate being, so complaint would be absurd. Alternatively 'heartless, witless' can be read as an angry reproach, identifying nature as alive and cruel. There is no resolving the ambiguity, and no need to, for Housman means both.

The simplicity of his technique brings home how baffling poetry is. The poem 'Into my heart an air that kills', for example, consists of forty-six perfectly ordinary words, used millions of times every day in innumerable permutations throughout the English-speaking world. Yet Housman takes them and puts them into a particular order, and lightning strikes. Something immortal is born. How? Why? No one knows.

His technical minimalism contributes to meaning as well as to style – and, typically, does so in two opposite ways. The choice of short, common words implies suppression of the ego. Splendour is shunned. Yet there is also something majestic about wielding such power while scarcely seeming to lift a finger.

Housman is easy to parody and hard to imitate. That is not surprising, for he was a rare and complex man: a professor of classics; a lifelong student of the textual intricacies of Latin verse; a sadistic critic of other scholars; a homosexual who responded to the legalized victimization of his kind with mingled guilt, shame, indignation and fury. So eccentric a profile might have made his poetry inaccessible to the mass of readers. But it seems clear that he strove to avoid this. Not that his homosexuality is hidden. It is explicit in poem after poem, and it is always a source of anguish, never of joy. The young men are shot or hanged or just wither away – re-enacting, it seems, the loss of Moses Jackson, the college friend who was the love of his life. But the pain the poems express is not specific to homosexuals. No one who has ever been hurt by love can fail to recognize it – the ache of absence, the stab of rejection. Equally real to today's readers is his liberation from the consolations of religion. His view of mankind is astringent in its courage and modernity. We are chance collections of atoms. At death we will disperse to the four winds. Others will think our thoughts and breathe the air we breathed. Our sense of distinctive selfhood is an illusion.

George Orwell
Coming up for Air
～1939～

George Orwell was a misfit by conviction. He saw that no one with a critical intelligence could be anything else. All his pre-war novels are about misfits, and *Coming up for Air* is the best. Its hero is George Bowling, a rep for the Flying Salamander Insurance Company. When we first meet him he is the possessor of a suburban semi (mortgaged), a nagging wife, a new set of dentures and a deep desire to get away. His chance comes when he wins some money on a horse. He tells his wife he has to go on a business trip to Birmingham, but instead takes a few days' holiday in Lower Binfield, the Thames Valley village where he grew up. He remembers it as a rural paradise of hawthorn hedges, wild peppermint and flowering chestnut, with two deep, secluded pools in the grounds of the old manor house where he fished for carp as a boy. But when he gets back there, the village has simply disappeared. It has been obliterated by thousands of new houses – Lancashire overspill. The pools have been drained and turned into rubbish tips. The river banks are black with people and gramophones. What was once clear water is thick with oil, pleasure boats and floating refuse. This is the first English novel to confront global pollution. There's no coming up for air, Bowling concludes, because there isn't any air. 'The dustbin that we're in reaches up to the stratosphere.'

Hardly a load of laughs, you might think. But in fact, thanks to Orwell's lugubrious wit and belligerent common sense, it is very funny, as well as invigoratingly realistic. Bowling shares many of his creator's grouses about modern life. There is a classic early scene where he bites into a frankfurter – a tricky operation with un-run-in dentures – and finds to his disgust that it is a new-style fish-filled sausage, a 1930s marketing wheeze that has fortunately not survived. Like Orwell, he finds the average contemporary British murder, as reported in the press, sadly inferior ('Not a patch on the old domestic poisoning dramas'). Like Orwell, he is quick to pounce on anyone mucking around with the English language. When his mother dies, the doctor tells him the growth was 'benign' ('which struck me as a queer thing to call it, seeing that it killed her'). There is a fine outflow of Orwellian bile when Bowling visits the old manor-house grounds and finds a select estate housing a colony of arty intellectuals – sandal-wearing vegetarians who fancy they are living the natural life ('It made me wish I'd got a hand-grenade in my pocket').

The most enjoyable bits are those that reveal Orwell as social historian, the observer of the common scene whose essays on boys' weeklies and seaside postcards established him as the unwitting founder of cultural studies. Bowling reminisces about pre-World War I sweets – Caraway Comfits, Farthing Everlastings, sugar mice at eight a penny. He also remembers how, for poor children, the seasons were marked by the supplementary diet they could glean from the hedge-rows: angelica in early summer, dewberries in July, sloes and hazelnuts in September ('Even plantain seeds are better than nothing when you're a long way from home and very hungry'). That reminds us that Orwell was also a keen naturalist – it was a facet of his unquenchable curiosity. Bowling's fishing gives him an interest in pond life – newts, water-snails, caddis-flies, leeches – and there is an episode where he muses on the mystery of their existence. You could spend a lifetime watching them, he thinks, and all the while you would feel inside you the 'peculiar flame' of wonder. 'It's the only thing worth having, and we don't want it.'

In the novel nostalgia collides with the nerve-tingling present. For Bowling – and everyone else – knows that war is imminent. He foresees the London blitz – even wants it to start, to end suspense. He is haunted by images of the totalitarian tyranny that, as Orwell rightly predicted, would swallow up half of Europe after the war. *Nineteen Eighty-four* is here in embryo. So is *Animal Farm*. At the end Bowling is startled to see a herd of pigs galloping towards him – only to realize that they are schoolchildren in gasmasks. Not many novels carry the seeds of two classics as well as being richly readable themselves.

Keith Douglas
Alamein to Zem Zem
~1946~

Keith Douglas was at Oxford when war broke out. He quickly enlisted, was commissioned in the Sherwood Rangers and posted to the Middle East. On 23 October 1942, when the Battle of Alamein began, he was in Cairo, seconded to Divisional HQ. Eager not to miss the action, he took a truck and, against orders, drove to rejoin his regiment. He served as a tank commander throughout the whole of the Allied advance across North Africa, and witnessed the German surrender in Tunisia. *Alamein to Zem Zem* is his story.

Boyishness and inexperience give it flashbulb immediacy. On his first day in action he notices a plane floating high above and watches a succession of silver droplets fall from it, as gracefully as a shower of rain. Just in time, he realizes they are bombs and dives into his tank's turret. The strange conditions of tank warfare are graphically conveyed. The regiment rides in Mark III Crusaders, low-slung tanks with long sloping lines that look like speedboats as they race across the desert trailing dust-clouds. Pulverized sand coats everything. Trucks, stores, tanks are dust-colour. Everyone wears a white dust-mask, like a clown. Wounds, even scratches, fester into monstrous desert sores.

An effect of the shattering engine noise inside the tank is that the world outside seems like a silent film. Men shout, vehicles move, shells burst, all soundlessly. Tank battles are remote and impersonal, like space wars. Douglas's first engagement happens when some blotches on the horizon, shivering in the heat haze, are identified as an enemy squadron. The whole regiment opens fire, Douglas feverishly loading rounds into the six-pounder while the turret fills with hot shell-cases. He sees nothing of the combat, learning only later that a victory has been won. The long periods of inaction add to the sense of detachment. For hours the tank crews huddle in their turrets, smoking, nibbling biscuits, reading. Douglas gets through a 'libraryful' of novels in the eight-month campaign.

Outside in the desert sprawl the dead, Germans, Italians, Libyans, New Zealanders, covered in flies. Douglas observes them in wonder, noting how their clothes tend to cover the places where arms or legs should have been, 'as though with an instinct for decency'. A company of Italian Bersaglieri lie 'like trippers taken ill', the breeze fluttering their plumed helmets, their corpses surrounded by picture-postcards of Milan, Venice, family snapshots, and other 'pitiable rubbish'. It was this kind of scene that Douglas immortalized in his most famous poem, 'Vergissmeinnicht'.

Loot is plentiful. As the retreating enemy vacate their positions, the tanks of Douglas's regiment take on cargoes of luxuries —crates of cherries, Macedonian cigarettes, cigars, straw-jacketed bottles of Chianti. Their commanders are festooned with Luger and Biretta pistols and German binoculars. 'We shared out the plunder with the immemorial glee of conquerors.' That rather grandiose appeal to history suggests a tinge of guilt. But you do not, as you read, begrudge them their pickings, because their zest is so understandable and their danger so acute. Sitting in a tank, packed with high-explosive ammunition and fuel, and being fired at, requires abnormal neglect of personal welfare. The effects of tanks burning punctuate the narrative with unforgettable scenes of horror.

Within the regiment, personal tensions crackle. The regular yeomanry officers are old-style country gentlemen, with a cavalryman's disdain for rules and procedures. They go to war fragrant with pomade, wearing suede boots, beautifully cut cavalry twill trousers, doeskin waistcoats, silk stocks with gold pins. Other ranks are treated with impeccable politeness, as if they were family retainers. Douglas, like the other new officers, fumes at these lordly throwbacks. Yet he respects them too, for they are utterly fearless and born to command. In his poetic tribute to them, 'Aristocrats', he celebrates them as unicorns – elegant, chivalrous, doomed.

There is no hatred for the enemy. Both sides treat prisoners well. Chatting with some, Douglas finds that one was at Cologne University and competed in athletics against Cambridge before the war. Another was an opera singer in Milan. Everything, from flowers carpeting the desert in winter to vanquished enemies, is seen with a poet's eye and the generosity of youth. Few battle narratives are so exuberant or so sensitive.

Despite being blown up by a mine at Zem Zem and briefly hospitalized, Douglas survived the campaign. He later took part in the D-Day landings. Three days after arriving in Normandy he was killed by a mortar bomb, aged twenty-four.

Thomas Mann
Confessions of Felix Krull, Confidence Man
~1954~

This is Thomas Mann's only comic novel. It shares themes with his serious work, but surrounds them with mockery. The effect is wonderfully enlivening – like chatting with a brainy friend after he has had a few drinks. Felix Krull, the hero, is a young man with the body of a Greek god and the morals of a bed bug. His father manufactures sparkling wine of execrable quality, so sumptuously bottled in a blaze of seals, monograms and silver foil that it is easily mistaken for a respectable beverage. This stands as a symbol for Felix, who esteems himself of finer clay than other mortals, but lacks any ethical sense.

A brilliant mimic, he learns as a schoolboy to append an exact replica of his father's signature to notes explaining his frequent absences. He drills his body to obey his mind, perfecting a technique for contracting and expanding the pupils of his eyes at will. This mental control proves invaluable when he reaches the age for military service. Earnestly protesting that he enjoys perfect health, he treats the medical board to a sequence of perfectly executed epileptic seizures and has to be forcibly ejected, still proclaiming his eagerness to join the German army.

Behind all this can be detected Mann's concern about the

artist as fraud and faker. Felix feels instant kinship with any-one who lives by illusion – actors, circus performers, prosti-tutes. Like Mann, he adores luxury. He educates himself by gazing into shop windows – florists, jewellers, vendors of exquisite clothes and leather goods. By patient study of these gleaming displays, he perfects himself in the refinements of a life that he cannot yet afford to live. His hedonism raises the question, fascinating to Mann, of how far art is identifiable with a sensuous reality deeper than words or morals. Felix is initiated into love by a prostitute called Rozsa, in whose com-pany he learns that words belong to the superficial realm of ethics, which is eclipsed by the inarticulacies of nature. Con-versation with Rozsa seldom progresses beyond simple, prac-tical directions, followed by cries of pleasure.

Moving to Paris, which he regards as the centre of the civi-lized world, Felix gets a job as lift-boy in a grand hotel. His beauty attracts lovers of both sexes, whom he satisfies as best he can. A wealthy woman novelist, masochistically enchanted to find herself in bed with a menial, begs him to whip her and steal all her valuables before he leaves. She is enraptured when he reveals that, before receiving this invitation, he had stolen her jewel case. More serious pleasure beckons when the young Marquis de Venosta, a guest at the hotel, persuades Felix to impersonate him. The Marquis's parents regret his attachment to an actress at the Folies Musicales, and have offered a fabulous world tour as an inducement to him to leave her. Instead, the Marquis remains secretly in Paris, pursuing his affair, and Felix, backed by the boundless de Venosta wealth, sets off for foreign parts disguised as the haughty young aristocrat. It is the moment for which all his training in fraud has prepared him. Menials and grandees alike are taken in by his patrician airs. His letters to the de Venosta parents are masterpieces of deception, perfectly imitating their son's style.

A fresh phase of adventure opens when he meets, on the train to Lisbon, Professor Kuckuk, a paleontologist, and Director of the Lisbon Museum of Natural History. The professor's explanations of cosmology and evolution display Mann's brilliance as a popular science writer and give the novel a whole new dimension. As in *The Magic Mountain*, though more light-heartedly, the human actors are now seen against the mind-shattering revelations of science, stretching from microbe to galaxy, on a time-scale that reduces human existence to a mere blip.

Some of this material, recycled in his own conversation, is of assistance to Felix in the difficult task of seducing the professor's daughter, the tantalizingly proud Zouzou. He is about to enjoy her equally desirable mother when the novel abruptly ends. Mann kept it by him for years, adding to it from time to time, but never finished it. That is no surprise. It is a novel you never want to stop reading, so stopping writing it would surely have been a wrench. Besides, there are intimations, in the part Mann did finish, that Felix will end up in prison – a gross moralistic absurdity which it is pleasing to think he could not bring himself to depict.

Kingsley Amis
Lucky Jim
~ 1954 ~

Quite a lot of people, especially, I have noticed, intelligent
women, detest this novel. They identify its hero, Jim ('filthy
Mozart') Dixon as a foe of high culture. They are right, of
course. But Jim's culture-phobia is not mere philistinism; it is
political. He hates the possessors of culture rather than culture itself. He belongs to the post-war generation that was
fired with hope by the 1945 Labour victory, but then watched
Britain slipping back into its old class-divisions, and culture
being reclaimed as the preserve of wealth and privilege.

Jim is a lecturer in medieval history at a provincial university, and the most prominent local representative of wealth
and privilege is his immediate overlord, Professor Welch, who
accordingly becomes the enemy. The Welches possess inherited money, maidservants, and the kind of big, rambling
house where you can give weekend parties and indulge in
string quartets and glee-singing. Their sons Bertrand and
Michel, respectively a painter and a writer, perpetuate the
combined soppiness and snobbishness of pre-war English
bohemia. Bertrand addresses Jim, a northern grammar-
school boy, as if he belonged to an inferior species. It is odd that
intelligent women do not sympathize with Jim more, for that

is exactly how Bertrand's many surrogates have traditionally addressed intelligent women. Jim is often accused of being anti-academic. But he is not. He believes in history being well taught. He despises Welch because he is the kind of smug, blinkered, inefficient freak (still observable in senior common rooms) who is useless in a university and unemployable outside one.

Not enough credit is given to Amis's writing about the opposite sex in this novel. It is one of the first attempts in English to describe women realistically. True, they are seen from an exclusively male angle. But that is how a realistic male must see them. Christine, the woman Jim eventually wins, is not the blonde bimbo critics write her off as. He registers her in carefully low-key terms. Her body feels 'rounded and rather bulky' against his when they dance. Her hair smells of 'well-brushed hair'. As often in real life, his longing for her is political as much as physical. She is from a class-level his type cannot normally aspire to, whereas Margaret, the frigid, dowdy bluestocking who has got her claws into him, and whom he mercifully manages to ditch, has all the marks of his destined mate.

What most readers prize in *Lucky Jim*, though, is not the politics but the humour – rightly, because humour can keep you sane whereas politics, as you only have to look around to see, generally have the opposite effect. Humour's sanity-preservation depends on its reworking the real world into disguises you can just about tolerate. Jim, with his silent yells of anguish and his repertoire of grotesque faces, spends a lot of time in this borderland between reality and fantasy, and the novel's great comic set-pieces progress from one to the other.

The episode where Jim, staying with the Welches, tries to eradicate cigarette-burns from his bedsheets with a razor blade, starts realistically and ends with him hacking huge, jagged holes in the hope that they might be taken for the ravages of monster moths. The excruciatingly slow bus-ride at the novel's end – which has strong claims to be the funniest passage of English prose – begins in sober exactitude and gradually levitates into comic extravaganza, with crowds of characters imported to maintain the fantasy – toddlers retrieving toys from under the bus's barely revolving wheels, knots of loungers parting unhurriedly at the touch of its 'reluctant bonnet'.

Throughout, it is the elegance and precision of the humorous writing that delights, and this matters because it smuggles a level of refinement into the novel that beer-swilling, fag-puffing Jim could not otherwise lay claim to. His sensations when he wakes up with a hangover provide the book's most beautiful sentence: 'His mouth had been used as a latrine by some small creature of the night, and then as its mausoleum.' The ascent here from the basic ('latrine') to the stately ('mausoleum') mirrors the flight into fantasy that the whole book endorses, and the tenderly poetic 'small creature of the night' seems to have strayed into the text from some quite uncomic provenance. The fact that thoughts like these occur to Jim is what wrong-foots the critics who want to denounce him as a philistine, and it convinces us that, despite his lapses, he has more right to be in a university than Welch.

William Golding
The Inheritors
~1955~

This is Golding's version of the Fall of Man, replacing the Genesis myth. It is also a serious piece of anthropological thinking. He sets it not in Eden but in the forests of prehistory. A group of Neanderthals are making their way, in spring, from their winter quarters by the sea to the lush green uplands. H. G. Wells, in a passage Golding quotes at the start, had conjectured that Neanderthals were probably gorilla-like monsters with cannibalistic tendencies. Golding's are different – innocent, peaceful, gentle. They are naked, but covered in glossy chestnut curls. Their bodies are beautifully agile, and think quicker than their minds. They eat the fruits of the forest, grubs, berries, fungi, honey. About meat, they have problems. They will eat it if it has been killed by something else – a sabre-toothed tiger, say – and will even chase off hyenas to get at the carcass. But they feel meat is wicked, and never kill another creature themselves, having, in any case, no weapons, only crude stone tools.

Their senses are as keen as a wild animal's, taking in the world as smells rather than sights. But their thinking-processes, like their speech, are slow and unfamiliar. They prefer to gesticulate and dance out meanings rather than using words, and they call thoughts pictures. 'I have a picture,' one of them will announce, meaning that an idea is forming, and the others are able, if they gather round and concentrate, to see the same picture in their heads. This thought-transference, together with their own special group smell, binds them together. Selfhood is barely conceivable. To be alone, away from the others' smells, is a terror. Among Neanderthals it is generally agreed that males are better than females at having pictures. But women alone have access to the true mysteries, for only they can make life. In their religion the creator is a goddess, Oa. She produced woman out of her belly, and woman brought forth man.

Golding takes us, with complete assurance, out of our own bodies and into this new world. We sense much of it through the nostrils of Lok, an adult male, who is not good, even for a Neanderthal, at having pictures, but is loved because he is a joker and a mimic. It is Lok who first meets the Other. It happens in the forest. The Other walks upright on spindly legs, and wears a mask of white bone. He smells of nobody. He holds out a tall stick towards Lok, as if he were offering him a gift. The stick bends, then straightens, and a tree beside Lok acquires a new twig that smells of Other and goose feathers and bitter berries that Lok's stomach knows are bad. Lok takes back the news: 'There are other people in the world.'

The Neanderthals' encounters with the new people, whom they spy on from trees and bushes, are all defamiliarized through this naïve perception. The new people have spears and knives, as well as bows and arrows. They cross water, terrifying to Neanderthals, in canoes. Their seeming masks are actually white faces. When they loosen a thong at their shoulder their skins slip off, leaving nakedness underneath. They are amazingly noisy, always laughing and talking. They make flat, dead animals on walls or the ground, using pigments. They get drunk. Their wine-skin baffles the Neanderthals, who take it to be a large wobbly animal making water into the new people's wooden cups. They have canine teeth like wolves, and they make love viciously as if they were fighting. They worship a male god in the shape of a rutting stag.

They are, of course, us – *Homo sapiens* – and for the Neanderthals their arrival is fatal. Tragically, the Neanderthals watch them with a kind of childish adoration, recognizing their superiority. But to the new people these strange, red-haired apes that spring from the forest are monsters, as they were to H. G. Wells, and they exterminate them. Only a Neanderthal baby survives, whom a female of the new people, having lost her own child, decides to keep as a plaything. Perhaps he will soon be sacrificed. Or perhaps he will grow up, mate and leave a redeeming trace of the innocent Neanderthal in our blood. For Golding, we are fallen because we are not Neanderthals – because, unlike them, we have big brains that wreck the world. It seems a likelier explanation than the apple and the snake.

V. S. Naipaul

The Mystic Masseur

~1957~

This was V. S. Naipaul's first novel. Like his other early work, it gave grave offence in his native Trinidad and shocked liberal-minded English reviewers. To make fun of an underdeveloped ex-colony was considered bad form – like bowling bouncers at tail-end batsmen. The patronizing assumption behind such protests was that Trinidadians, being naturally inferior, should be exempt from satire. Naipaul disagreed. His account of the island's social customs – the popularity of wife-beating, even among wives; the high regard for quacks and charlatans – is devastatingly funny. The banquet at Government House, at which the newly elected members of the Legislative Council and their wives come up against the challenge of Western cutlery and eating habits, is a comic *tour de force* and also, depending on whether you laugh, or sweat with embarrassment, a reliable indicator of your post-colonial guilt.

The distinction between Western enlightenment and third-world ignorance is less clear-cut in early Naipaul than it became later. Nothing in *The Mystic Masseur* is simple. The central figure, Ganesh Ramsumair, remains an enigma. You cannot be sure what is going on inside him, or how you are meant to respond to his meteoric career. Educated at Queen's

Royal College (the school Naipaul attended), he is a mediocre student but falls in love with books. Oil-company royalties on a piece of land left him by his father allow him to amass a collection of Penguins and Everymans that awes his illiterate neighbours. He develops a connoisseur's appreciation of typefaces and paper-smells (Harrap's French–English Dictionary being the best-smelling book, in his view). The idea of becoming a writer possesses him, an ambition strangely unconnected with the actual business of writing.

Much of this fits Naipaul's account of his own boyhood. Being a writer was for him, too, 'a fantasy of nobility', linked vaguely to ideals of justice. But whereas Naipaul left for Oxford on a Trinidad Government Scholarship, Ganesh sets up as a healer. The business does not thrive, partly because Ganesh has no healing powers, partly because the village where he lives, Fuente Grove, is a wretched huddle of shacks, surrounded by miles of sugar cane, which anyone seeking health would instinctively avoid. One day, however, a mother brings her son to be healed. The boy has been pursued by a black cloud ever since his younger brother, going on an errand in his stead, was killed by a truck. Ganesh questions him, lays on an elaborate ritual, and effects a complete cure, seemingly by magic but actually by intelligence and do-it-yourself psychotherapy. The news spreads and immense success follows. Lunatics of all kinds flock to have their demons cast out. Fuente Grove becomes a health resort. Taxis (in which Ganesh prudently acquires a monopoly) import battalions of servicemen from the American bases, hungry for native culture. Ganesh builds a Hindu temple and a mansion, equipped with the triumphs of Western technology, including a musical toilet-paper rack that plays 'Yankee Doodle Dandy' when you pull a sheet.

He is not exactly a fraud. He helps the poor and teaches the parity of all religions. To his disciples, he dispenses the wisdom of Everyman and Penguin. But the book that brings him the widest fame is his own. Entitled *What God Told Me*, it begins: 'On Thursday, May 2, at nine o'clock in the morning, just after I had had breakfast, I ṣaw God . . .' We never learn whether this vision is genuine, nor what beliefs, if any, propel him into politics. He becomes the most powerful member of the Legislative Council, an MBE and a stout defender of English colonial rule. In a prophetic parody of Naipaul's own development, he turns into a perfect replica of an English gentleman and insists on being called not Ganesh Ramsumair but G. Ramsay Muir, Esq.

Naipaul dedicated *The Mystic Masseur* to the memory of his father and his father's shadow lies behind it. Naipaul senior had been a reforming journalist on the *Trinidad Guardian*, but also a student of mysticism and religion. His son sensed some deep hurt or shame in him, but found out only long after he died that he had been the victim of a witchcraft conspiracy. He was threatened with death and forced to sacrifice to the goddess Kali, whose cult he had mocked. When Naipaul wrote *The Mystic Masseur* he knew none of this. But the character of Ganesh, modernist and mystic, perhaps reflects the inscrutability that he found in his father.

S. J. Perelman
The Road to Miltown, or Under the Spreading Atrophy
~ 1957 ~

S. J. Perelman was a master stylist as well as a comic genius. All thirty-four pieces in this collection (reprinted, mostly, from the *New Yorker*) are bravura displays of style, and each gets its buzz from sending up someone else's idea of what is stylish. Like magic beanstalks, the individual items start from almost nothing. A pretentious snippet from *Harpers* or some other glossy is enough to set him off. An ad for boneless veal steaks, for example, in which a smug cutlet is presented eulogizing its own tenderness, inspires a full-scale domestic drama (entitled 'De Gustibus Ain't What Dey Used to Be'), where a tape-recorder concealed in the Perelman icebox discloses a whole colony of loquacious foodstuffs, woundingly frank about the human menage. A Hathaway shirt commercial, lauding the gritty virtues of a Scots weaver of shirt fabrics, grows into a Perelman playlet, set in a Highland glen, where a rain-sodden posse of Hathaway executives strive to ingratiate themselves with a mean and humourless Caledonian peasant.

Nationality clashes, cheerfully guying racial stereotypes, are a Perelman stand-by. A news item, mentioning that Pandit Nehru is in the habit of sending his laundry to Paris, prompts an exchange of letters in which the Indian leader complains of damaged underthings in elaborately insulting public-school English, and a cringing Gallic *blanchisseur* responds. A book-piece from the London *Times*, tinkling with belletristic whimsy about the joys of reading while on an ocean voyage, is countered by a surreal Perelmanian adventure in north Borneo, where the headman of the Dyaks paddling the canoe proffers a volume of recent British humour retrieved from the bilge ('You catchum plenty bellyraffs along him. Hot off the pless').

As this exchange suggests, Perelman kept a weather eye on English writing. But his mixture of slang and elegance is all his own. The nearest match this side of the Atlantic would be P. G. Wodehouse, who was as fine a stylist, but hamstrung by innate British flunkeyism and class-worship. The New York glimpsed through Perelman's sketches, by contrast, is bracingly egalitarian. Bootblacks and bartenders break in on his meditations with pointed disrespect. His newsvendor, reprimanding him for failing to collect a copy of the *Journal of Heredity* he has ordered, scans the contents page suspiciously and lights on an item investigating cannibalism in mutant mice. As Perelman grabs his periodical and flees, discussion of his moral character is already under way ('Cannibalism in mice. Jeez, no wonder a woman ain't safe on the streets').

Ten of the pieces are about old movies which were landmarks of Perelman's youth and which he has recently taken a second look at in the projection room in the Museum of Modern Art.

These excursions into early autobiography are winningly self-mocking. Mesmerized by a movie version of *Twenty Thousand Leagues Under the Sea*, twelve-year-old Perelman wades into the ocean in a diving helmet improvised from a lard pail, a length of hose, and a bicycle pump, which a friend on shore manfully plies. A passing fisherman hauls him aboard just in time. Later his tastes refine. The spectacle of Gloria Swanson in Cecil B. De Mille's *Male and Female* has him declaiming romantic avowals to the chickens as he feeds them their mash. Enchanted by the Prussian hauteur of Erich von Stroheim in *Foolish Wives*, he takes to clicking his heels and enunciating '*Bitte?*' when introduced to fellow sophomores, while screwing an imaginary monocle into his eye. The general tenor of all ten pieces is that, viewed a second time, what had once seemed classics of filmic art turn out to be abject codswallop.

This pleasingly illustrates how much more foolish and gullible the young are than their elders – a truth not much emphasized nowadays. Even more enjoyable are Perelman's barbed resumés of the offending films, which contain enough snappy putdowns to last most critics a lifetime. Memories of his own days in film are dotted around. The Marx brothers, for whom he wrote scripts, flit in and out. A director, battering on his door at 3 a.m., delivers a reproach that one longs to reuse in similar circumstances: 'Crisake, are you in bed already? What are you, a farmer or something?' Some strange self-mutilating impulse on the part of publishers has prevented this book appearing in England. This may seem to make it an inconsiderate inclusion in my list. However, you can buy second-hand copies of the New York edition on the internet – and it is worth the trouble. I rate it among the three or four wittiest books ever.

W. H. Auden

Collected Shorter Poems 1927–57

~ 1966 ~

People tend to think of Auden as a Marxist poet of the 1930s. But he was much bigger than that. His poetic ambition was to map the world – not its geographical surface, but the inner terrain of fears and desires we journey through every day of our lives. The landscapes he created to symbolize this region changed with time. The early poems recall the moors and derelict mine-workings he explored as a boy in Yorkshire, transforming them into a mysterious territory of spies, frontiers and fortified farms that reflect the tensions of the inter-war years. Later, a different cast of characters moved in – lions, witches, beggars, cripples, bears, woodcutters – from Freudian dream-psychology and folk-tale.

The magnitude of his enterprise was matched by the authority of his poetic voice. Certainty was his great gift, which is strange when you consider how little he thought we could be certain of. His pronouncements resound like edicts, providing watchwords to live by. 'Evil is unspectacular, and always human', for example, is a judgement that reshapes the whole moral universe. 'Poetry makes nothing happen' is a dictum constantly quoted in debates about literature – usually by people who do not reflect that poetry is making them quote it, so proving the line's untruth. He seems capable of saying the last word on any subject. His sonnet about biography ('A shilling life will give you all the facts') reads like the essence of all biographies. His 'Epitaph on a Tyrant', though written specifically with Hitler in mind, holds true of all tyrannies:

When he laughed, respectable senators burst with laughter,
And when he cried the little children died in the streets.

A factor that gives the poems power is their wide-angle consciousness. They seem aware of what is happening not just in their vicinity but everywhere. The elegy for W. B. Yeats, one of Auden's poetic peaks, has its receptors open to a whole continent:

> *In the nightmare of the dark*
> *All the dogs of Europe bark ...*
> *Intellectual disgrace*
> *Stares from every human face.*

It is as if the earth were under surveillance from some Olympian spy-satellite. 'Hong Kong', another 1930s poem, fills in its political context with majestic nonchalance:

> *off-stage, a war*
> *Thuds like the slamming of a distant door.*

The late poems can be just as breathtaking in their scene-changes. Some stanzas about the fall of Rome shift, without missing a beat, thousands of miles:

123

> *Altogether elsewhere, vast*
> *Herds of reindeer move across*
> *Miles and miles of golden moss*
> *Silently and very fast.*

These amazing blips of perspective involve time as well as space. What other poet, watching holidaymakers on the beach at Dover, would think of the age of the sun?

> *tides warn bronzing bathers of a cooling star*
> *With half its history done.*

When space-travel at last allowed astronauts to look back at the earth, and watch the 'great swatches of plankton' move through the oceans, Auden was captivated. But he had been doing it for years without the aid of technology.

It is this awareness of elsewhere that inspires his greatest poems. 'Musée des Beaux Arts' ('About suffering they were never wrong,/The Old Masters') tells us that individual tragedy is, however heart-rending, insignificant to most people. Every personal catastrophe is surrounded by vistas of inattention. The dogs 'go on with their doggy life'; the torturer's horse 'Scratches its innocent behind on a tree'. His love-poem 'Lullaby', which must surely be among the half-dozen poems from this century that will last as long as people fall in love, gains its unique poise and maturity from the recognition of love's smallness and temporariness against the infinities of space and time.

> *Lay your sleeping head, my love,*
> *Human on my faithless arm.*

Already in that second line the perspective has shifted from tenderness to doubt. As the poem goes on the cries of 'fashionable madmen' and the disasters prophesied in 'the dreaded cards' darken the vision. Love fades, dwindles, is engulfed by the devouring world. It is because the poem cherishes what it has despite this that it is so moving. It makes the best of things – like Auden's version of Christianity which counsels:

> *Love your crooked neighbour*
> *With your crooked heart.*

A warning. Throughout his life Auden altered, pruned and discarded poems. His mid-life change from Marxism to Anglo-Catholicism intensified this self-censorship. Some supreme poems ('Spain 1937'; 'September 1, 1939') are missing from this volume because Auden decided they were 'trash'. Critics have lamented this. But instead of feeling peeved it is more appropriate, surely, to marvel at the integrity that could scrap such treasures.

Günter Grass
The Tin Drum
~1959~

Before he wrote *The Tin Drum*, Günter Grass was unknown. His one success had been winning third prize in a regional poetry competition. The novel caused an uproar. In Germany it was denounced as likely to 'endanger, if not destroy, the human soul and mind'. There were many attempts to ban it. To Germans eager to forget their past, Grass seemed criminally irresponsible, retelling in loathsome and malignant detail the years of Nazi rule. His very choice of narrator appeared insulting. The story is told by a scabrous midget, Oskar Matzerath. To outward appearance a child of three, he has a fully developed adult brain and libido, and a fine gift of irony. He gains a privileged insight into the lives of grown-ups because, regarding him as an innocent toddler, they perform their most intimate functions in his presence.

His special gift is that his screams can shatter glass – teachers' spectacles, tumblers, shop-windows – and he is a compulsive drummer, needing a constant supply of toy tin drums which two weeks' use reduces to scrap metal. In this figure Grass found a voice equal to the crazy abominations he had to describe. Like his creator, Oskar is born in Danzig and is five when the Nazis come to power. He watches his fellow citizens eagerly adapting themselves to the new order. On Kristall-nacht, in November 1938, when Jewish businesses were wrecked, he comes upon his favourite toy-shop owner dead in the excrement-daubed ruins of his shop. Ten months later, Oskar and his father are among the defenders of the Polish Post Office building when the Nazis blast it into subjection. They find time, amid the mayhem, for a bizarre card-game, in which one of the players bleeds to death, still clutching his cards.

During the war Oskar travels to France with a troop-enter-tainment company, arriving in Normandy just in time for the Allied invasion. But he is back in Danzig when the Red Army liberates the city. As the Russian soldiers come clattering down the cellar steps, Oskar's stepfather desperately tries to swallow his Nazi Party badge, chokes on it, and is riddled with bullets by one of the liberators who takes his agonized throat-clutching dance as some kind of hostile display. Oskar's cool irony is equal to every horror. The great love of his life, a dwarf actress, is with him in Normandy when the Allied bombardment begins, and running over to the field-kitchen in her high-heeled shoes 'reaches the steaming-hot coffee at exactly the same time as a shell from a naval gun'.

The supporting characters are richly lifelike, reminding us how improbable human beings can be. There is Greff the pae-dophile greengrocer, a whiz at mechanical gadgetry, who hangs himself on a carefully contrived musical gallows, and Meyn, the trumpeter, who joins the Hitler Youth band, earns commendation for destroying a synagogue, but is expelled, with impeccable Nazi logic, for cruelty to cats.

Grass originally planned his monster novel as a series of poems, and its sensuousness can be overwhelming. In one notorious sequence Oskar and his mother are strolling by the Baltic when a fisherman hauls out a horse's head crawling with eels. This may allude to the doomed Polish cavalry, one of the novel's recurrent symbols. But for the reader the main problem, as the fisherman proceeds to squeeze the eels out, is how not to be sick – an effort beyond the power of Oskar's mother, who brings up her copious cooked breakfast, to the satisfaction of the screaming gulls who devour it. Grass's sensuousness can delight as well as nauseate. Oskar's keen nostrils distinguish women mainly by their aromas. Maria, his step-mother and bedmate, smells of wild mushrooms and vanilla and – after Oskar, in imaginative foreplay, has poured raspberry fizz powder into her navel – of raspberries. Oskar, like Grass, is reared in a family grocery store and its mingled smells – herring, kerosene, dried fruit – lie deep in his psyche.

Grass, in this novel, pioneered 'magic realism'. Modern practitioners of the genre often seem to choose it for no better reason than that they cannot manage realism. With Grass, though, it makes his writing more realistic, not less, and answers the demands of his subject. He makes you feel that to speak of the events he covers in a level, prosaic voice would be indecent, because it would be to accept them as sane. His writing – exorbitant, tumultuous, anarchic – is a living rejection of the 'forces of order' Nazism represented.

Muriel Spark
The Prime of Miss Jean Brodie
~1961~

If a cat could write novels, they would be like Muriel Spark's. That is meant as a compliment. Cats are subtle, elegant, reserved and free from any foolish sentimentality about human beings. What makes them most Sparkish are the lethal talons they keep politely out of sight in their velvet pads. Behind Spark's purring ironies you sense something equally implacable. Critics sometimes relate it to her Catholicism. But in *The Prime of Miss Jean Brodie* that does not obtrude much, yet the same chill is felt.

No book was ever less like the popular image of it. People think of Miss Brodie as jolly and rather lovable – an admirer of Hitler and Mussolini, but an inspiring teacher, and rightly proud of her pupils as the '*crème de la crème*'. When you read the book, it is not that these judgements are proved wrong, rather that you are left completely in the dark about what judgements, if any, to make. The presentation of Miss Brodie is rigidly external. She might be a bug or a butterfly for all you see of her thoughts. You hear her mesmerizing her class with romantic spiel about Italian Renaissance art, her holiday in Egypt, and her fiancé Hugh who 'fell on Flanders field'. You learn, from whispered rumours, of her love for the art master Mr Lloyd, whom she renounces (because he is married?

because he is a Catholic?), and of her affair with Mr Lowther the music teacher. Throughout, Spark scrupulously withholds either praise or blame. Sandy, the pupil of Miss Brodie's we come to know best, believes that Miss Brodie may be one of the damned. There is a 'whiff of sulphur' about her. But Sandy is going through a Calvinist phase and could be exaggerating.

It is Sandy who eventually betrays Miss Brodie – reporting her Fascism to the headmistress and getting her sacked, to the delight of the jealous pack of inferior teachers. Is this right or wrong? Sandy has little piggy eyes. She looks, we are told, untrustworthy. Unlike Miss Brodie, she makes no bones about having an affair with married Mr Lloyd. Later she becomes a nun, but even that seems dubious. She finds in the Catholic Church 'a number of Fascists much less agreeable than Miss Brodie'. So should we admire Sandy or not? It is impossible to tell. Impossible, too, to feel affection for her or anyone in the book. In another writer that would matter. But in Spark the remorseless detachment is what holds you spellbound.

It is at its most disturbing when, in the middle of some light-hearted scene between Miss Brodie and her pupils, we are suddenly swept into the future and told of the fates that will overtake the characters. We learn that Miss Brodie will die of cancer just after the Second World War, while still in her fifties. We even hear one of her pupils, now grown up and married, say she is going to put flowers on Miss Brodie's grave. These God's-eye glimpses of futurity strike like blasts of Arctic air, withering the lives we are watching. The cruellest of them relates to a lumpish, stupid pupil called Mary who, we are told, will die at the age of twenty-three in a hotel fire, running up and down a blazing corridor, the noise of the flames drowning her screams. This uncannily mirrors an earlier scene. In a science lesson the girls do an experiment with lighted strips of magnesium, and Mary, panic-stricken, runs up and down between the benches surrounded by flames. Is this coincidence part of some sinister divine joke? Does fate punish Mary because she is stupid? The troubling implications are eminently Sparkian.

Miss Brodie's girls, simmering with sexual excitement and ignorance, are believable and wonderfully funny. Sandy and her friend Jenny write a novel about Hugh in which he is not killed after all, but returns from the war, believes Miss Brodie loves another and retires to a mountain eyrie where he holds Sandy and Jenny captive ('His black eyes flashed in the lamplight of the hut'). They also compile a series of love-letters from Miss Brodie to Mr Lowther, using phrases culled from newspaper reports of sex cases, which they take to be the way adults talk about love ('I may permit misconduct to occur again from time to time'). The absurdity should make us reflect that we are not much better equipped than Sandy and Jenny to say how the grown-ups really talked when they were alone together in this inscrutably feline book.

Jean-Paul Sartre
Words
~1964~

Distilled from one of the bleakest brains of the century, this childhood memoir hides pain behind its wit. The wit makes it irresistible; the pain, human. Sartre's father died when he was two. His mother, Anne-Marie, nursed her husband devotedly but, Sartre reports, 'did not carry indecency so far as to love him'. Given that he was an infant at the time, this prim little joke can scarcely be based on actual knowledge. But he needed to believe it, because it sustained his Oedipal passion for his mother, which is the book's core. He wanted to think her entirely his – a scarcely tarnished virgin, yielded up to him by his father's fortunate death.

The bereaved mother and child went to live with her parents. She was penniless and jobless, and for Sartre this reinforced the illusion that she was just a child like him. They shared jokes, myths, private fantasies. Bath-time was a pre-pubertal erotic paradise, fragrant with soap and eau-de-Cologne. Quite soon, in fact, his mother married again. Her new husband was a philistine scientist, impregnably rich and successful. Sartre's detestation of him and his bourgeois values helped to make him a Marxist. But *Words* mentions none of this. The mother–child idyll is preserved, innocent, crystalline, poised on the edge of disaster.

Apart from his mother, the dominant influence was his grandfather, Charles Schweitzer, a grandiose figure with a flowing beard. Family legend had it that one day he entered a church through the vestry while the priest was threatening the faint-hearted with celestial thunder: 'God is here! He is watching you!' Suddenly the congregation saw, beneath the pulpit, a tall, bearded old man eyeing them. They fled. To his grandson he was enthralling – so much so that what he said scarcely registered. 'I was too busy listening to hear.' The intensity of what adults take to be childish inattention, caught in that memory, is typical of Sartre's uncanny reconstruction of childhood. He distinguished men and women, he recalls, partly by smell – the men's smells being less pleasant but more serious. Their repulsiveness was part of their glamour. Contrasted with his mother's delicate scent was the halitosis of his schoolmaster, M. Barrault, which little Sartre relished as the odour of learning and virtue.

Despite the adoration of his mother and grandparents, he was an ugly child, almost a dwarf, with a wall eye. Other children shunned him and banned him from their games. The pain of exclusion is what his wit has to surmount. His mother had allowed his curls to grow to hide his ugliness. But his grandfather, denouncing effeminacy, took him to a barber and had him shorn. Even he was aghast at the result: 'He had taken out his wonder child, and brought home a toad.'

Like many lonely children Sartre sought self-oblivion in

books. He read everything from Buffalo Bill to the Grand Larousse encyclopaedia with fanatical zest. The dawn of literacy has never been described more ardently. Compared with the vitality he found in books, everyday life seemed a cemetery and the human heart insipid. Soon he was writing fiction himself, in a volume labelled 'Exercise Book for Novels'. The cinema was another escape. His mother took him and they gloated together in the warm dark. The films were silent, accompanied by a piano. When they got home she would play the piano and little Sartre, armed with his grandfather's paper knife in lieu of a rapier, would act out feats of daring, opening and shutting his mouth silently like his screen heroes.

Sartre meant *Words* to be a renunciation of his earlier self and his middle-class family culture, viewed from the vantage-point of Marxism. 'I loathe my childhood and all that remains of it.' But the memoir belies that. His mockery is affectionate. He remembers how, with precocious insincerity, he would simulate a model child at prayer, hands demurely clasped, 'waging a titanic struggle against pins and needles'. He smiles at his juvenile faith in human progress: 'Progress, that long and arduous road that led to myself.'

His grandfather's joy in his grandson's young life was, he now realizes, a kind of acceptance of death. Like the old man's love of mountain tops, waves and stars, it was a way of embracing that nature that was about to reclaim him. *Words* is full of such human insights. They have little to do with Marxism, or its alternatives.

Seamus Heaney
Death of a Naturalist
~1966~

This was Seamus Heaney's first collection. Unlike most poets, he did not start versifying as a teenager. A farmer's son, born in Mossbawn, County Derry, he felt remote from the literary world. 'I had some notion that modern poetry was far beyond the likes of me – there was Eliot and so on.' By contrast with the modernists, he aimed, when he began writing poems as a schoolteacher in Belfast, to be understood by ordinary people. His subject matter was ordinary too – butter-churning, potato-digging, the daily routines of the farm. But to most poetry readers these topics are far from usual. They shine with the glamour of a rural past, sturdier and more valid than modern life. This loamy rootedness has helped to give Heaney's poetry its feeling of moral integrity.

As a countryside poet, he might be expected to fit into the tradition of the English Romantics. But in fact he reverses that whole tradition. Whereas the Romantics' urge is upward and ethereal – Shelley's skylark, Keats's nightingale – Heaney's is downward. He delves into mud and slime. His childhood memories are forays into life's squelchy, putrid, decaying underside. He culls the 'thick slobber' of frogspawn from a festering flax-dam, where monstrous, cacophonous frogs, 'their blunt heads farting', are the 'great slime kings'. He remembers an oily stretch of river out of which a villainous, grey-snouted old rat 'slimed'. The volume's last poem, 'Personal Helicon', considers his childhood obsession – his passion for wells and water-holes, for fingering slime and snuffing up decay – and concludes that being a poet is the adult equivalent. Seeing his face reflected in those rotting depths was like descending into the mystery of himself. So, too, is writing poetry:

> *I rhyme*
> *To see myself, to set the darkness echoing.*

The mud-fixation that distinguishes Heaney from the Romantic poets marks him as post-Freudian and post-Darwinian. Before Freud, the ultimate realities were always upwards. When you died, your soul went up to heaven, where God was. But Freudian psychoanalysis digs down through life's accumulated layers to find the real – the repressed trauma that has directed all subsequent growth. A poem written for his wife Marie, at the time of their wedding, acknowledges that a child still 'diligently potters' in his brain, 'puddling through mud in a deep drain'. In its wedding context, this hints at a sexual connection between mud and the female. Mud-dabbling, it is suggested, was a kind of pre-sexual sexual play, and in Heaney's later poetry Marie becomes explicitly a 'polder' or mud-bank.

Digging down through geological strata was the path to truth for Darwinism too. Moreover Darwinism posits, as the origin of human life, not fully grown, walking, talking proto-types, fresh from the hand of God, but bits of slime in which somehow living cells formed. At some point in the Darwinian progress from slime to us, mind, consciousness and language developed. Heaney's poetical descents into slime retrace that trajectory. His poetic language seems, too, to want to revert to something physical rather than mental. It is not just that he assembles a burly squad of monosyllables – 'squelch', 'pus', 'slap' – that simulate primitive speech. Rather, he can, more than any poet since Keats, inject words with weight and texture.

Scrabbling among muck and decay suggests death as well as nascent life, and Heaney's poetry richly associates the two. The Danish peat-bog corpses became a central symbol in his later work. *Death of a Naturalist* inspects death with juicy zest – from the 'rat-grey fungus' on rotting blackberries, to the dishonoured carcass of a Christmas turkey – 'a skin bag plumped with inky putty'.

But the finest poem in the book, Heaney's early master-piece, 'Mid-Term Break', is in a plainer mode. About coming home from boarding school for the funeral of a small brother, knocked down by a car, it is watchful, calm, scrupulously real-istic. His mother, he noticed, did not exactly weep but 'coughed out angry tearless sighs'. The child's body showed 'No gaudy scars, the bumper knocked him clear'. It is this acute fidelity to the unsensational that has made Heaney our foremost living poet.

Stevie Smith

The Frog Prince and Other Poems

~1966~

On the poetry-reading circuit in the sixties Stevie Smith would pose as a crazy old bat, reciting 'Not waving but drowning' in a quavery voice. The disguise pleased her because it eschewed pomp. But it hid her keen intellect and artistic originality. To escape the solemnity that she associated with male authority, she patched together a new poetic idiom out of bits of nursery rhyme, nonsense verse and Grimms' fairy-tales. Through this seemingly innocent prattle, her own insights jab. Her drawings illustrating the poems practice the same sly subversion.

Her ideal is not 'sloppy' romantic togetherness but a lonely, educated life, watchful and critical, recognizing that the price of intelligence is seeing through other people. Her Frog Prince is not sure he wants the princess to come and disenchant him. He has been quite happy as a frog. Smith, nodding by the fire with her cat, cherishes the thought that the apex of creation is simply 'Cat, night, fire – and a girl nodding'. Fear of being lonely betrays women, she sees, and selfish men unerringly choose mates who will 'cherish them and be neglected and not think it inhuman'. Reading about the illegitimate birth-rate in a newspaper –

> *Oh, girls, girls,*
> *Silly little cheap things*

– she urges them to:

> *put some value on yourselves,*
> *Learn to say, No.*

She links them with another newspaper item about a panther that briefly escaped its cage. Its 'angry and innocent eyes' seem to say 'I am too valuable to be kept in a cage' – and that is how girls should react to the risk of being trapped in mother-hood. If they did, and everyone learned to respect everyone else as valuable, it would be good, she predicts, for panthers too.

She does not underestimate the dangers of loneliness. Sui-cide was always on the cards – 'I keep casting loving looks at the gas oven,' she joked. But she believed suicide a right to be stoutly defended, not a danger. Like solitude, it was an escape from 'distractions and the human crowd'. Death was a friend who would end 'the nerviness'. Maybe this, as well as her poetic virtuosity, recommended Smith to Sylvia Plath, who confessed herself a 'desperate Smith addict'. On this topic, and others, she fell foul of Christianity and its 'demonic urge to boss'. Its anti-feminism ('How cruel is the story of Eve') and its meaningless dogma riled her. In a brilliant nonsense poem she encounters some sinister children who proclaim, as an article of faith, 'Our Bog is Dood' and threaten to crucify her if she disagrees. Religion, with its dreams of power, seemed to her a typically masculine invention. 'To feel trivial and idiotic, and to live with this feeling, is to be a hero in a way that no God can be'. The people and animals in her poems often feel like this, though some try to hide it, like the Dedicated Dancing Bull:

> Ho ho, thump thump
> Oh I am elegant, oh I am plump.

She did not hate men. Their power, she thought, was to their disadvantage as well as woman's:

> Man, poor man,
> Is he fit to rule?

Pretentiousness, in the poems, is commoner in women than men. A drawing of a wild-eyed intellectual-looking female is accompanied by a poem recalling her conversation:

> She said everything is swimming in a wonderful wisdom
> Silly ass.

Men are more often just selfish. Stevie's father abandoned his wife and two daughters when Stevie was a baby. Her mother and Stevie's 'noble aunt' from Hull struggled to rear them and send them to good schools. Several poems celebrate the 'house of female habitation' where they grew up – 'A house expecting strength as it is strong', counting despair derisory, stern and reserved but warm at heart. These values pass into the poems. So does the education the girls received. Reading them, you are expected to be able to translate snatches of

French, German and Latin, to pick up allusions to Homer or Racine's *Phèdre*, and to appreciate the odd bilingual joke –

> *Ceux qui luttent ce sont ceux qui vivent*
> *And down here they luttent a very great deal indeed.*

None of this was meant to be exclusive. It was the kind of knowledge any sixth-former of Stevie's generation had. Educated, fastidious, self-reliant, pessimistic, scornful of celebrity and glamour, these are poems healthily at odds with our current beliefs.

Ted Hughes
Crow: From the Life and Songs of Crow
~1970~

Crow is Hughes's most powerful work. He described its language as 'super-ugly', and it gives you the sense of standing close to something very dangerous, a furnace door, or some deafening piece of machinery. It was written in the aftermath of tragedy. Its dedicatees, 'Assia and Shura', were Hughes's mistress Assia Wevill and their two-year-old daughter, whom she killed when she killed herself. But its outcry is not just personal. A document of the Cold War, it anticipates nuclear holocaust. A post-Christian testimony, it confronts man's universal loneliness. Its scenery is both cosmic and corporal. Worlds end, stars fume away into blackness, and the human body bursts into a butcher's shop of horrors.

What saves it from mere despair is Crow. Obscene, indestructible, screaming for blood, brutally funny, he is Hughes's own creation, not drawn from any previous myth. His job, on the contrary, is to destroy any mythical underpinning we might have imagined life had. His very being is anarchic. Now fool, now victim, now hoodlum, he does not possess a coherent personality, and his surreal adventures – of which this is just a selection – will not fit into a consistent narrative. His brushes with the Christian God are farcical, and not to God's credit. In Eden, while man's and woman's bodies lie inert, without souls, God nods off. Crow intervenes, bites the snake in two, stuffs the tail half into man, with the wounded end hanging out, and the head half into woman, where it peers out through her eyes, calling to its tail half to join up. So the trap of sex is sprung, God continues to doze, and Crow exits laughing. In 'Crow's First Lesson', God tries to teach Crow to talk – '"Love", said God. "Say, Love".' Crow gags, retches and coughs up first a shark, then a swarm of blood-seeking insects. In Crow's universe, Love is a nonsense-word. The deaths of innumerable other creatures are written into every creature's survival pack. But when Crow feels guilty about this –

> Alas ought I
> To stop eating
> And try to become the light?

– his qualms are reduced to nonsense too. The universe is not only irredeemable. There are no redeeming attitudes to strike.

All man can be certain of, in this extreme, are the laws of science, and his own wish that something existed beyond them. The world is a machine. Crow, standing by a stream, recognizes it as a small, auxiliary motor fastened to the 'infinite engine' that takes in the whole earth and the heavens:

> littering away
> Beyond every limit.

Watching a battle, Crow sees it as the operation of inexorable

143

mathematical principles. Men are wrenched in two by theorems, they shriek from sudden onsets of calculus. Bullets pursue their courses:

> Through intestines, pocket-books, brains, hair, teeth,
> According to Universal laws.

As for moral or metaphysical truths, Crow finds no vestige of these in the material world he forlornly dissects. He plucks grass-heads and gazes at them, 'Waiting for instructions'. He finds a dead mole and takes it apart, 'Then stared at the gobbets, feeling helpless'. The desire for supernatural certainties, which no other animal shares, is exposed in *Crow* as one component of the human catastrophe. Another is language which, as Hughes sees it in *Crow*, is an escapist illusion that replaces reality with words. The effect is fatal, for language turns itself into beliefs and slogans for which men slaughter one another, until the globe is:

> *a brittle desert*
> *Dazzling with the bones of earth's people.*

Humanist commentators, worried by the poems' blackness, have combed *Crow* for signs of hope. They have suggested that mother-love is a positive, and it is true that Hughes pursues mother-goddess dreams elsewhere. But in *Crow* the mother is just another trap. Crow tries to escape her, but she keeps getting in the way. He drives off in a car and finds the tow-rope is round her neck. He jumps into a plane, and her body is jammed in the jet. Eventually he takes a rocket to the moon, crashes on its surface, and crawls out 'Under his mother's buttocks'. The originality of these poems lies precisely in their not endorsing the values, hopes, affections and beliefs we already have. It cancels all those, exposing them to the relentless searchlight of cosmic reality. In exchange it offers only its own black humour which, if comfortless, is at any rate illusion-free.

Ian McEwan
The Cement Garden
~1978~

Horror in English fiction is traditionally shrouded in Gothic gloom. Ian McEwan replaces that with clarity. Each sentence is as neat as the cubes of colour in a child's paintbox. Yet cumulatively they lead to depths from which mind and body recoil. Horror is never the main point, however. An aggressive intelligence drives his narratives, demanding that we re-examine our ideas about 'natural' behaviour.

In *The Cement Garden*, his first novel, the narrator is Jack, a fourteen-year-old, preoccupied with acne, serial masturbation, contempt for his father and other routine interests of adolescence. He has a small brother, Tom, and two sisters, Sue, younger than him, and Julie, who is beautiful and the eldest. Their house is the sole survivor in an urban wasteland. All the streets around were demolished for a motorway that never got built. Now it stands alone except for some distant tower blocks. This isolation is vital for McEwan's plot, and is intensified by the children's parents, an ingrown, querulous couple without friends or living relatives. The father, a control freak with a weak heart, is intent on cementing over the garden to make it tidier. But the strain of humping the cement-bags up from the cellar kills him off in the first chapter. After that, the family draws in on itself even more. The mother, ill and exhausted, takes to her bed, and their occasional drab celebrations, such as Jack's fifteenth birthday party, are held around it.

When she dies, the question of what to do confronts the children. McEwan's solution, for all its weirdness, seems completely convincing, like an experiment in behavioural psychology for which the conditions have been carefully set. They never think of getting help, or letting anyone take their mother away. She belongs, they assume, with them. Burying her in the garden is a possibility. But they fear they may be overseen from the tower blocks. So they encase her in freshly mixed cement in a large metal trunk in the cellar. The secret binds them closer, and sharpens their mutual tensions. As usual in McEwan's stories, the females prove tougher than the males. Julie slips naturally into the mother's role. Poised and mature, she lies out in the garden in her bikini sunning herself (the school holidays have begun) and acquires a boyfriend, Derek, a professional snooker-player. Sue escapes into words, writing letters to her mother as if she were still alive. Tom, desolate, regresses. He decides he does not want to be a boy any more, and Jack watches, strangely excited, while the girls dress him in a cut-down frock, topping it off with a curly wig. Within weeks Tom has drifted back to babyhood, carried around by Julie, and put to sleep in a cot at night.

Between Julie and Jack, relations are more difficult, and McEwan pursues them with tense care. She has outgrown him, and her womanhood makes him feel lost, inferior and aroused. His one advantage is his physical strength. Violence threatens when he finds a sledgehammer in the undergrowth. But she distracts him by allowing him to rub sun-lotion into her back and legs. At last, inevitably, they seek comfort in each other's arms and Derek bursts in on a scene of tender, mothering incest. Because Derek is smug and shallow, his outrage points us towards other possible reactions. In earlier centuries the developments we have watched – fierce family solidarity, sibling incest, infantilism – must have been common and sanctioned ways of dealing with the anguish of bereavement. Though the police and social services who are about to arrive as the novel ends (summoned by Derek) will no doubt sort things out according to their own hygienic rules, the children, it could be argued, have coped more supportively with orphanhood than our culture allows. No social worker could give Jack Julie's sisterly love.

McEwan could not prompt such thoughts if he did not enter so accurately into the ordeal of growing up. There is a moment early in the novel when Jack, having left for school, slips back to peer through the window and sees his mother clearing away the breakfast things. The realization that she goes on having an independent existence while he is away brings a feeling of 'sadness and menace, in unbearable combination'. These buried wounds that adulthood ices over open unfailingly at McEwan's touch. They are his gateway to truth.

Clive James
Unreliable Memoirs

~1980~

As a pupil at Sydney Technical High School, Clive James survived by storytelling. Not being large or athletic, he had to hone his defensive skills and he found that his sheer verbal artistry could keep whole packs of thugs agog. It was the best possible training for authorship. He writes like a man who knows he may be torn to pieces if he lets boredom supervene for a microsecond. He is the kind of stylist who does not just cross Niagara on a tightrope. He cycles across, backwards, juggling. His prose is like petrol thrown on a slumbering bonfire. You marvel, re-reading *Unreliable Memoirs*, at how ordinary the materials are. Nothing much happens. He grows up in a dim Sydney suburb called Kogarah, graduates from Sydney University, does his National Service. But the way he tells it, it becomes a spellbinding comic saga, now violent, now elaborately poetic, like a Tom and Jerry cartoon crossed with a baroque cathedral. Just describing the colours and flavours of the brands of sweets which kids at the Kogarah Odeon's Saturday morning sessions would buy, devour and throw at each other becomes a high aesthetic adventure.

He is a master of build-up. When *aficionados* mull over their favourite passages, you notice how much they lose if they are not perfectly memorized. Highspots like the near-death of grandpa James from swallowing a festive sixpence in a mouthful of Christmas pudding, or the drama of the billycarts which Kogarah's youngsters race down its steeply banked pavements, and which, under James's leadership, they bolt together to form a single monster suicide-cart, are as finely wrought as filigree. Change a word and they crumble. You might as well tamper with the syntax of *Paradise Lost*.

On your first read-through you may be laughing too much to notice the generosity. But it matters. Stories that might be cruel are saved by their warmth. As a vacation job, he becomes a bus conductor on one of Sydney's busiest routes. In the commuter-crush he unknowingly closes the automatic doors on the neck of an elderly lady about to board. Her head and hat, decorated with wax fruit, are inside the bus. Her body, gamely trotting to keep up and carrying a shopping bag in each hand, remains outside. The yells of fellow passengers eventually stop the bus – and James's career as a conductor. But it is the lady's niceness that stays with you. She apologizes for causing so much trouble. This raconteur, you realize, is, for all his mockery, in love with Australia and its people. Even its military. His bugbear in basic training is a permanently screaming, physically hideous sergeant major. But during a weaponry session an inept recruit drops a mortar bomb into the mortar nose-first. While the rest of the squad take to their heels or try to burrow into the ground, James's bugbear calmly lifts the mortar, shakes the bomb out, and replaces it the right way up. 'We all marched thought-fully back to camp.'

Behind it all lies tragedy. When James was a year old, his father went away to fight in the Second World War. He was captured by the Japanese, but survived. At the end of the war the plane bringing him home crashed in Manila Bay, killing everyone aboard. The spectacle of his mother's grief, James thinks, marked him for life. It is easy to believe. His feats of delinquency, comic only in retrospect, come across as attempts to punish his mother for her attachment to a dead hero. Her bewilderment at her son's perversity accompanies the narrative like a continuous muffled scream. When, in 1961, the liner taking James to England edges away from the quayside, and the coloured streamer he has thrown to his mother taut-ens and snaps, he is still wondering whether she sees, at the far end of it, her husband or her son.

But the book's splendour outshines its sadness. It is sumptu-ously sensuous. He remembers a friend's mum giving them buttered bread with hundreds and thousands on it, 'like a slice of powdered rainbow'. He hymns the Australian rabbit, a mobile banquet of sweet white flesh, 'like a dryad's inner thigh'. You gasp at each new conceit, wondering, as the playground mob at Sydney Tech must have, whether Jamesie has at last over-reached himself. But, like them, you come back for more.

John Updike
A Rabbit Omnibus
~1991~

Updike's Rabbit saga is often praised as a lifelike portrait of middle-America in the second half of the twentieth century. That should give grave offence to middle-America. Harry ('Rabbit') Angstrom, Updike's hero, is a perpetual adolescent, selfish, lecherous, irresponsible, and not much good at anything. Aged twenty-six when the story begins, he once knew glory as a high-school basketball star. But that golden age is now yellowing press-cuttings, and he demonstrates kitchen gadgets in a department store for a living. He has a son, Nelson, and an alcoholic wife, Janice, whom he spends most of volume one on the run from. He returns when she bears him a daughter, but she accidentally drowns the baby in the bath while drunk. With the second volume the sixties arrive and Janice gladly embraces the catchwords of liberation. In search of personal validity, she shacks up with a Greek car salesman, while Rabbit welcomes into his home a black activist junkie sought by the police, and a stoned young socialite, Jill, who drives a Porsche and denounces materialism. White neighbours express their disapproval of these unusual house-guests by burning down the Rabbit residence and Jill is incinerated. When volume three opens in 1979, Rabbit is back with Janice, and rich, having inherited his father-in-law's used-car lot and Toyota agency. Nelson has dropped out of college and is about to become a father. The volume peaks with Rabbit and Janice taking a wife-swapping holiday in the Caribbean with two other couples.

Decay is everywhere. Brewer, the industrial city in Pennsylvania where Rabbit lives, was never a thing of beauty. Its shoe factories and bottling plants replaced fields and farms. But at least it was prosperous. Now it is in decline. Spaces where children played are given up to vandalism and terror. Older residents decry insurgent Blacks and Hispanics. The trilogy's twenty years cover Vietnam, campus riots, the oil crisis. The American dream has soured. Rabbit's parents were serious, upright folk, church-goers, who bought day-old bread to save cents. By contrast, his son Nelson is a spoiled, weak, vicious runt for whom religion is garbage and education a waste of time. Modern America, as illustrated by Rabbit's friends and relations, is coarse, ignorant, philistine, foul-mouthed, arrogant, cultureless, infantile and sex-obsessed. Worse, it rules the world. When the gasoline dries up, Nelson relishes the prospect of nuking the Arabs. The book's version of American values is epitomized when Rabbit and Janice convert part of their fortune into Krugerrands and excite themselves by having sex on a bed strewn with gold.

So why choose this book, given that its events and people are sullying and obscene? Updike's writing is why. Each page is a cascade of delicately caught sense impressions – from the scratch of a key in a lock to the ghostly rings left by glasses on a table. The human body is an unending challenge and wonder for Updike. No writer has ever described the myriad appearances of flesh with such devotion – puckered or apple-smooth, sun-warmed or moistly private, aroused or withered or dead. He captures the arbitrariness of human perception – the hundreds of meaningless photos snapped by the memory. He is the laureate of consumerism, enthralled by gadgets and commodities. For Rabbit – or Updike – a bathroom medicine-cabinet is an Aladdin's cave, each packet and bottle secluded in its special aura. He writes a couple of sentences about a tube of toothpaste, and you feel you have never looked at one before. A car's tail-light, smashed in a collision, becomes a symphony of glittering plastic shards and colour-coded wiring.

His appetite for incidentals rewrites social history. He studies the décor of restaurants, or underwear design, or the area of pubic hair in *Penthouse* centre-spreads, and comes up with new ways of mapping the progress of our culture. True, he is a poet moonlighting as a novelist, so there is a chasm between what he sees and what we can credit his characters with seeing. The intense poetic life of his writing could not conceivably reside between the ears of Rabbit or Janice or Nelson, who never read a book and whose imaginative worlds are bounded by TV and booze. All the same, his tireless mission is to transfigure the commonplace, and show how, with a small adjustment of the lens, it can become beautiful. Even Rabbit gets an inkling of this at times. 'What a threadbare thing we make of life,' he ponders. Updike repairs the threads.

Philip Larkin

Collected Poems

~1988~

Readers of Larkin's poetry tend to feel they have a personal relationship with him. That is unusual, and unfashionable. T. S. Eliot decreed that poems should be impersonal. But Larkin's often read like diary entries. He notices wedding-parties on station platforms, or visits an empty church while out cycling, and we are inclined to believe that he actually did these things. When his letters were published some readers, discovering that his political views differed from theirs, felt betrayed, as if a friend had let them down. That was simple-minded, of course. Yet it tells us something about the poems. The personality they project – wry, unpre-tentious, adult – gains our trust. It needs to do so, because, despite his reputation as Mr Glum, he is a didactic poet, teaching us how to survive.

His birthday wish for Kingsley Amis's new-born daughter is that she should be 'ordinary' –

> *If that is what a skilled,*
> *Vigilant, flexible,*
> *Unemphasised, enthralled*
> *Catching at happiness is called.*

No lines better express his stance. His alleged pessimism is a warning against humanity's perpetual golden dream of perfection, which kills our pleasure in the real. This is the glamorous never-never land that advertisers lure us to believe in, ridiculed in the poem 'Essential Beauty'. It is also the mirage of sexual triumph in the brain of the rapist in 'Deceptions', bursting into 'fulfilment's desolate attic'. But though Larkin scorns the vanity of human wishes, he does not scorn the wishers. He understands the pain that drives them to want to escape from their lives. The elderly women in 'Faith Healing', convulsed by helpless, ugly sobs, are in the grip of the same false hope that all of us cherish:

> In everyone there sleeps
> A sense of life lived according to love.

Our visions of happiness make us miserable because we believe they could have come true – which is like looking at the past, 'blindingly undiminished' in photographs, and believing that 'By acting differently we could have kept it so'. A skilled, vigilant catching at happiness demands we see through these deceptions, as Larkin does in 'Toads' and 'Toads Revisited' – classic statements of the humour and resignation he requires us to share with him.

Catching at happiness in Larkin's way does not eradicate the sadness from life. It recognizes it as what happiness has to be wrung from. Poised and self-aware, it rejects sentimentality. When the horses in 'At Grass' 'gallop for what must be joy', the over-eager phrasing reminds us that their imagined joy may just be our wishful thinking – they may gallop from habit, or boredom. At the end of 'An Arundel Tomb' our glad assumption is even more sombrely checked. The couple hand-in-hand on the grave monument prove:

> *Our almost-instinct almost true*
> *What will survive of us is love.*

In a more naïve poet the last line would be triumphant. In Larkin, the previous line has already withered it with truth.

Though the poems teach us disillusionment, they do not despise innocence. 'MCMXIV', the poem about volunteers queuing to enlist for the Great War, looks back to an England happier than ours, and its innocence was part of its happiness. So too in 'Church Going' there is no pretence that we are better off because we have lost the consolations of religion. They answered a need we still feel. To see that, and to see we cannot assuage it, is to be grown-up. When the church has vanished and is just a patch of brambles, people will still gravitate, Larkin predicts, to this 'serious' place where 'so many dead lie round'. He does not share their superstition, but nor does he blame it.

Fear of death runs through the poems, and is presented as universal. The whole intricate edifice of civilization is identified as 'the costly aversion of the eyes from death'. Such terror may seem irreconcilable with Larkin's poised realism. But on the contrary, to admit terror is to refuse self-deception, as realism demands. The poems are wise enough, too, to acknowledge that death is not just feared but desired. To call it:

> *the solving emptiness*
> *That lies just under all we do*

is to grant that it will solve as well as dissolve. The poem 'Wants' frankly recognizes Larkin's yearning for solitude as a version of the death wish: 'Beneath it all desire of oblivion runs'. Self-knowledge as the goal of life is as old as Socrates. Larkin re-writes it for our time.

Vikram Seth
A Suitable Boy
~ 1993 ~

Vikram Seth's mammoth novel about newly independent India challenges comparison with *War and Peace*, and does so knowingly. The wolf-hunt in *A Suitable Boy* clearly mirrors the wolf-hunt in Tolstoy's epic, and Tolstoy's technique of mediating huge political events through the fortunes of a small group of families is adopted by Seth. Both novelists have an uncanny gift for characterization, creating people so real and engaging that you speed-read to see what happens to them next. Seth's daring extends to his choice of subject. There is no topic on which enlightened English people feel more superior to Indians than that of arranged marriage. The idea of being forced into wedlock outrages our strongest liberal instincts. So when Mrs Rupa Mehra, widow of a civil engineer, forbids her daughter Lata's love for the dashing, cricket-playing Kabir, simply because he is a Muslim and she a Hindu, and plans to marry her instead to paan-chewing Harish, who works in the leather trade, we are programmed to react with horror. Yet we do not. For so skilfully does Seth convey Mrs Mehra's essential goodness that our urge to condemn is replaced by understanding. The problem of arranged marriage is rescued from the unreality of moral prejudice and reinvested with human complication.

The same personal depth animates the novel's politics. Large tracts of the book are taken up with verbatim reports of debates in the Legislative Assembly about the bill to deprive hereditary landowners of their estates. It is hard to think of another novelist who could make such material readable. But with Seth the abstract issues are absorbed into an intriguing network of personalities, feuds and grievances.

The savagery and injustice endemic to Indian civilization are not downplayed. The obscene ferocity of racial massacre and the lightning speed with which it erupts, the city slums oozing black filth, the ignorant, brutalized village communities, mired in corruption, the sickening cruelties visited on outcastes if they venture to claim rights as human beings – we witness these. But despite them the novel's overwhelming feeling is buoyant. People are warm, courteous, playful and vividly contrasted. The Chatterji family with their in-jokes and banter are set against the old-money refinement of the Khans. Snobbish Arun Mehra, Mrs Rupa's eldest, is opposed to his likeable, incompetent brother Varun. Mrs Rupa's father, Dr Kishen Kand Seth, is a walking contradiction, ferocious and sentimental by turns.

The folk festivals, the religious processions, the intricate, sensuous traditions of classical music and song, the curiously Indian fusion of pomp and informality, make English culture seem drab by comparison. We are engulfed by Seth's India, its vastness and endless variety, its temples, hovels and rambling ancestral palaces, its jacaranda, jasmine and bougainvillaea, its saffron-clad sadhus, naked pilgrims and diamond-studded rajahs with rose-petals strewn before their feet, its smells of incense, marijuana and sweat. Through it all flows the sun-burnished holy Ganges, bearing away the ashes of the dead.

But the English inheritance is powerful too. Lata is studying English Literature at university. Her brother-in-law Pran teaches it. The syllabus committee's meetings, with diehard Professor Mishra blackballing James Joyce, are richly comic and believable. The ruling genius of this sumptuously Indian novel is not a many-handed goddess but an English provincial spinster of the eighteenth century, Jane Austen. Lata is reading *Emma*, and the friction over her playing Olivia to Kabir's Malvolio in *Twelfth Night* echoes the fuss about amateur dramatics in *Mansfield Park*. Seth's values are Austen's. When the brazen Meenakshi, Arun's wife, has the gold medal which her father-in-law won as an engineering student, and which Mrs Rupa entrusted to her as a wedding-gift, melted down to make ear-rings, the vulgarity of the act carries the same moral opprobrium that it would in Austen. What is demanded of Lata, if she accepts her mother's advice and marries Harish, though still in love with Kabir, is a rejection of passion in favour of reason that reflects the cool-headed stance of Austen's *Sense and Sensibility*.

This preference resonates in the political spaces of the novel. Passion is to blame for the tragedy of partition, and for the spectacle of Hindu and Muslim mobs hacking each other to pieces. The same irrationality, of course, lies behind Mrs Rupa Mehra's prejudice against Kabir, which Lata's obedience condones. The novel cannot conceal this unrightable wrong, however warmly it solicits our sympathy and affection. It exasperates even as it charms, which is why Lata's fate grips us to the very last page.

Kazuo Ishiguro
The Unconsoled
~ 1995 ~

This novel is about stress, a problem of epidemic proportions
in our culture that modern fiction largely ignores. Ishiguro's
previous books were realistic accounts of how the past haunts
the present. With *The Unconsoled* he broke through the realism barrier and plunged into inner space. It starts realistically.
Ryder, an internationally celebrated pianist, arrives at a hotel
in an unnamed central European city to give a recital. He has
only hazy memories of his schedule and the young woman
assistant allocated to him by the Civic Arts Institute proves
elusive. He is greeted everywhere with effusive courtesy, but
learns with mounting consternation of promises he has broken and appointments he has failed to keep. He gathers that
the concert at which he is to perform will be the climax of a
cultural controversy that has divided the city, upon which he
will be expected to adjudicate.

It soon becomes clear that we are in a region between dream
and waking. Ryder, weighed down by his mysterious respon-
sibilities, hears conversations at which he is not present, and
reads anxieties in others people's minds. His hotel room curiously resembles a bedroom he had as a child. Strangers in the
street metamorphose into school and college acquaintances.

The hotel porter Gustav has a grown-up daughter, Sophie, and it gradually dawns on Ryder that he has lived with her as man and wife and that her son Boris is his child.

As the complications multiply, Ryder is swept by tides of panic and anger. Buildings and districts transmute bewilderingly. He finds himself trudging through muddy fields, descending dizzying staircases, stepping through doors into fantastic interiors. Events conspire to thwart his preparations for the concert, and he is terrified it will be a disaster. People persist in telling him, at nerve-jangling length, of their private problems. Their pleas for help spark frenzied guilt and impatience. He is drawn into a bizarre scandal centring on Brodsky, a drunken ex-conductor, and the fastidious Miss Collins, allegedly Brodsky's wife. Like many of the book's entanglements, this generates scenes of hysterical comedy, in which toe-curling embarrassment and grotesque personal mishap are narrated in Ishiguro's gravely courteous prose.

Ishiguro is adept at revealing the despair locked within human beings. It seeps through their conversation like blood through bandages. How hard it is for children and parents to show love to each other is a constant theme. Gustav and Sophie, though devoted to each other, are not on speaking terms. Hoffmann, the impresario behind the concert, expects his son Stephan to atone for his own artistic shortcomings and cannot forgive him for failing. Ryder's own parents are a source of deep agitation. He wants them to witness his triumph at the concert and badgers his hosts about arrangements for their reception. But seemingly there was never any chance of their attending. The roots of stress in the expectations parents burden their children with are shown, too, in Ryder's relations with Boris. The depiction of the juvenile male, at once timid and engrossed in violently destructive daydreams in which he heroically protects his elders, is sharply real. Ryder's coldness towards the child is met with ingratiating displays of pleasure that are infuriating to Ryder because he sees them as patently false. Our love for children or parents is, Ishiguro implies, indissolubly linked to a wish to have them different.

Though the book may cause puzzlement at first, once you have got used to its ruptures of reality it becomes tense and absorbing. The method, something between Kafka and *Alice in Wonderland*, allows Ishiguro into recesses of the subconscious closed to ordinary fiction. Figments and realities are not distinguished. On several occasions Ryder is able to hear both the flattering courtesies lavished on him by his admirers and the insulting comments about his vanity and egotism that they exchange between themselves. Whether these criticisms are actually audible or only imagined by the neurotic Ryder is a question the book's surrealist technique does not allow you to ask. For that matter you cannot tell whether anything in the book takes place outside Ryder's mind. That justifies the technique. For it is a symptom of stress that it cannot tell true from false fears. It is an endless battle with phantoms that may be actual. A realist novel about stress could not show this. Ishiguro must take us beyond realism to write realistically about it.

Graham Swift
Last Orders
~ 1996 ~

Graham Swift's 1996 Booker Prize winner, the last of my fifty choices, looks back across the century. Ray, Lenny and Vic, three regulars from the Coach and Horses pub in Bermondsey, are on their way to Margate to fulfil the last wish of their old mate Jack, which was to have his ashes thrown into the sea from Margate pier. Vince, Jack's stepson, is driving them. Ray is an insurance clerk and a serious student of the turf; Lenny is in fruit and veg; Vic is an undertaker. Jack owned a butcher's shop, and wanted Vince to go into the family firm, but Vince had classier ideas and now sells luxury cars to oil-rich Arabs. As they make for the coast in Vince's blue Mercedes, Swift unreels their past lives in snatches of talk and internal monologue. Now one of them, now another, takes up the narrative, passing it round as they pass round and nurse on their knees the plastic crematorium jar holding what is left of Jack. In flashbacks, Jack and his wife Amy add their voices to the gathering memories.

It is the wartime generation Swift celebrates. Jack and Ray were at El Alamein together, and Jack saved Ray's life. Lenny was a gunner, Vic served with convoys. They spent their youth in a pastoral England quite close in time but unimaginably different from ours. Jack and Amy met on a hop-picking holiday in

166

Kent. Ray's old man was a scrap merchant with a cart-horse called Duke which hauled a wagon round the Bermondsey streets. (Ray remembers that it was sitting beside his dad, watching Duke's backside, that first gave him thoughts about women – a connection typical of the book's fascination with how the mind knits itself.)

Seemingly artless, but as precise as a string quartet, the story gradually fits together. Just before war broke out, Jack and Amy had a daughter, June, who was born brain-damaged. She is still alive – now a woman of fifty – in an institution, but has never shown the least flicker of mental awareness. Twice a week, without fail, year in year out, Amy has visited her, hoping to stir some sign of recognition. But Jack has never been able to acknowledge her existence or hear her name mentioned. The bitterness that grew between Jack and Amy carried benefits for others. At the end of the war they adopted baby Vince, whose family had been wiped out by a flying bomb, to fill the gap left by June. Later Ray, ever the opportunist, waylaid Amy on one of her hospital-visiting days, and they had a short but blissful affair, consummating their love inside his camper-van at a number of classic race-meetings while the crowd roared outside.

The intimacy and depth of the writing imprints each character indelibly – Jack, dying of stomach cancer and sprouting plastic tubes, still chatting up the nurses; Vic savouring the secrets of the undertaker's craft; Lenny, an ex-boxer, needling Vince who, years back, got Lenny's teenage daughter pregnant and threw her over. Vince is the hardest character to like, but the book's generosity extends even to him, showing us behind the spiv a bewildered child, laughed at at school, and an adolescent unwillingly tangled in Jack's and Amy's grievances. What they are all trying to do is take in the ungraspable fact of death – a subject too old, you would think, for novelty, yet Swift addresses it with searching freshness. Ray, at the crematorium, feels that none of it has anything to do with Jack – the velvet curtains, the flowers, the music. 'I stood there, looking at the curtains, trying to make it have to do with him.'

The novel's hero is the English language as spoken by ordinary people. There is not a phrase you might not hear in a Bermondsey pub any night of the week. Swift's own voice never interposes, and the connectives in the dialogues are kept basic ('I said . . . He said . . .'). Yet the effect is profoundly elegiac, proverbially wise, as rhythmic as the surge of waves. Shakespeare occasionally gives lower-class characters speeches that shame the high-ups by their gentleness or nobility. But here that effect is carried through a whole book. Cockney speech becomes a vehicle for nuance and tenderness. If a language reflects the temper of its people, we should be proud of this book's language – or proud of the generation, now passing, that spoke it.

Afterwards

A Books-Choice Postbag

Choosing favourite books is a game all readers like to play, as I soon found out. Letters began to arrive shortly after my first column had hit doormats. The ones I liked best were chatty and nostalgic, recapturing those special moments of discovery that give perspective to life, and that only the bookish can have. 'Thank you for sending me back to a book first read in a tent in Saudi Arabia, 23 December 1947'; 'I discovered S. J. Perelman some forty years ago in, of all places, a bin of second hand books on display in a Catholic church in Chittagong, Bangladesh' (this from a 'blissfully certified Perelmaniac').

Suggestions for books unaccountably omitted from my list were numerous. One reader offered his own list of fifty which overlapped with mine in only two instances, Yeats and Hasek. (A more sceptical correspondent demanded 'Do you honestly like Hasek consistently? All the way through? As a re-read?'). Why, I was asked, had I not included Yutang Lin's *Gay Genius*, or Kurban Said's *Ali and Nino*, or Jean-Pierre Greenlaw's *The Coral Buildings of Suakin*, or K. Dhondup's *The Water Horse and Other Years: A History of 17th and 18th Century Tibet*?

Because I had never heard of them was, of course, the answer, and my respect for the erudition of *Sunday Times* Books Pages readers, already high, soared. A reader who approved of my reviving undervalued authors – Chesterton, Bennett – pressed the claims of R. C. Hutchinson, a novelist, as he pointed out, loaded with praise in his day by such panjandrums as J. B. Priestley and Hugh Walpole. Hutchinson, C. S. Lewis averred, was one of the very few living novelists who would be read 'fifty perhaps a hundred years hence'. A warning against making book-choices.

Thomas Hardy's poetry was a popular inclusion. One reader who applauded it was a poet himself, and sent me a copy of his first collection. Bulgakov's *A Country Doctor's Notebook* also scored. A retired professor of English, grateful for the introduction, rated it 'quite unparalleled'. But among the plaudits there were stern rebukes. 'I feel that the fame and respect that you won by the publication of *The Intellectuals and the Masses* has been thrown to the winds by your choice of the fifty books for the millennium.' Mercifully this prefaced a rather mild letter, which took serious exception to only two of my choices, Kingsley Amis ('that boorish drunk and bore') and George Orwell ('the fellow is vastly overrated'). Disagreement about these two was interestingly common. One reader explained that he had 'just taken the typewriter out of storage' to tell me about a friend who was turned off reading for life by being made to study Orwell ('a bore and a fraud') at school. But another had cured his 'lifelong prejudice against Orwell' by reading *Coming Up for Air* at my suggestion. Amis had passionate defenders as well as detractors. Readers prompted by my list to give *Lucky Jim* a try expressed elation: 'Does any novelist possess the integrity and sense that Amis does?', 'How did I miss reading it?! A secondhand copy kept me entertained for several days.'

Some readers had fascinating insider knowledge. Prompted by *Goodbye to All That*, the widow of a contemporary of Robert Graves, who entered Charterhouse in the same year, wrote about her husband's war. He was shot in the head ('I have his helmet with bullet hole'), but survived to spend a happy life farming in New England. Sylvia Townsend Warner's literary executor wrote to say that *Mr Fortune's Maggot* had a particular personal importance for its author because, unlike Mr Fortune, 'she spent her life trying not to change those she loved'. Keith Douglas's *Alamein to Zem Zem* produced the most exciting letter of all. 'I met Douglas in Alexandria before Alamein when he was engaged to my cousin Milena Pegna.' The writer went on to explain that Milena, whose breaking off of her engagement to Douglas inspired some of his finest poetry, was not the 'siren' some have made out, but a gentle, sensitive girl who did not feel ready for marriage. 'On the very day I read your column Milena died in Sydney aged 79.'

Unexpectedly, it was my piece on Aldous Huxley's *Those Barren Leaves* that brought the zaniest responses. I had innocently suggested that the relation between mind and matter was still an open question. A Fellow of the Interplanetary Society wrote to say this was incorrect, and proceeded to explain it himself in three unintelligible pages. Another well-wisher shared with me his homely recipe for reconciling God and Einsteinian physics. 'It's like putting a pair of trousers on $E=mc^2$ and saying "That's my Dad, that is".'

Two letters came from prison. One outlined the difficulty of getting adequate texts to study Ted Hughes's *Crow* in Park-hurst. The writer had, nevertheless, notched up several A-levels, including English, and was beatifically uncomplaining: 'I'm just an elderly convicted armed robber who deserves nothing.' The other was from a student I taught when I had a temporary job at Christ Church, Oxford, forty years ago, who is now serving a life-sentence. His string of crimes included torturing a rival art dealer, and the judge described him as 'highly dangerous'. Not a good advertisement for the human-izing effects of English Literature. Or perhaps I did not teach it properly. More cheering were two enormous letters, packed with book-chat, from the owner of a CD store called Tom's Tracks in Providence, Rhode Island. Despite regretting my 'occasional lapses into academic esoterica like Empson', the sender was jubilantly appreciative and divulged that since July, when he found he could no longer get through to the *Sunday Times* website, he had driven a considerable distance each week and paid ten dollars for the paper, just to get hold of my column. Editor, please note.

The shortest letter was from a Fellow of Clare College,

Cambridge, who pointed out that Housman's 'Into my heart' has forty-six words, not forty-eight as I had alleged. He added, kindly, that my effort was 'otherwise excellent'. The most heart-warming was from a reader in Hildersham who said that for him 'The series has rekindled the joy of good reading'. I walked a little taller that day.

Acknowledgements

I would like to thank the *Sunday Times* for permission to reprint these essays. It was Geordie Greig, Literary Editor at the time, who first suggested I should write them. I am deeply grateful for his enthusiasm and encouragement.